The Road to Resilience

From Chaos to Celebration

Sherri Mandell has known unspeakable horror in her own life. She has listened to the pain of countless others and has helped them. She has gained a thorough and thoughtful command of the ever-expanding body of literature on the subject. With this book, she has coupled her experience and expertise with her masterful literary skills to present a heartrending masterpiece. Read it. You will weep, but you will learn to hope. You will come to appreciate the capacity for resilience with which all human beings are endowed.

RABBI DR. TZVI HERSH WEINREB

Sherri Mandell has written a most compelling book – powerful in its unflinching honesty, its confrontation with pain and loss, and its groundbreaking definition of resilience. Her call to use the grief we all must experience in our lives as a springboard for personal growth reverberates long after the last page is turned. The author clearly has lived each of the seven spiritual steps she teaches, adding immediacy and poignancy to a book that is a magnificent gift to each and every reader. A life-affirming work.

DR. AVIVA WEISBORD

In this extremely valuable book, Sherri Mandell shares a deep wisdom forged by the searing experience of the murder of her son. Her insights into the growth potential inherent in tragedy are illuminated by wisdom from Jewish texts and psychological research on trauma, as well as her work in helping thousands of bereaved families find their own path to resilience. I strongly recommend this book, not only for those going through difficult times such as illness, divorce, or bereavement, but for anyone who seeks a deeper understanding of how to deal with life's challenges.

DR. DAVID PELCOVITZ

The Road to Resilience is a moving and very instructive read. With grace, beauty, poetry, and surprising humor, Sherri Mandell shares hard-earned wisdom for weaving life's tragedies into song. Marvelous and inspirational, moving and insightful, spiritual and practical; the minute I finished reading it I wanted to pick it right back up and start again.

TODD SALOVEY

Sherri Mandell

THE **ROAD** TO **RESILIENCE**

From Chaos to Celebration

The Toby Press

The Road to Resilience
From Chaos to Celebration

First Edition, 2015

The Toby Press LLC
POB 8531, New Milford, CT 06776–8531, USA
& POB 2455, London WIA 5WY, England
www.tobypress.com

ISBN 978-1-59264-383-7

A CIP catalogue record for this title is
available from the British Library

Printed and bound in the United States

For my husband and children:
You are my blessings.

Contents

Three ways are open to a person who is in sorrow. One who stands on a normal rung weeps, one who stands higher is silent, but one who stands on the topmost rung converts sorrow into song.

Rabbi Menachem Mendel of Kotzk

There is a story, always ahead of you, barely existing. Only gradually do you attach yourself to it and feel it. You discover the carapace that will contain and test your character. You find in this way the path of your life.

Michael Ondattje

Where is God to be found? In the place where He is given entry.

Rabbi Menachem Mendel of Kotzk

Preface

The Jewish people are masters of resilience. Throughout our history, we have undergone massacres, pogroms, inquisitions, wars, the unspeakable destruction of the Holocaust, the first and second intifadas in Israel, war with Hamas in Gaza, and still we prevail, maintain our dignity, and thrive. Not only as a nation, but as individuals. In fact, in a recent international survey, Israelis were rated some of the happiest people on earth.

Vitka Kovner, who along with her husband, the great poet Abba Kovner, fought in the resistance in Europe during the Holocaust, told me that after the Second World War, she and her husband and their comrades who had survived the war considered traveling back to Europe to avenge their losses by poisoning the water supplies or engaging in other acts of sabotage. They knew, though, that rather than focus on destruction, it was more important to build the Land of Israel.

I can attest to the power of Judaism and the Jewish people to support and sustain in times of difficulty. My son Koby was thirteen years old when he and his friend Yosef Ish Ran cut school and went hiking in the Haritun Canyon near our home in Israel. The two boys were murdered by Palestinian terrorists on May 8, 2001 – trapped in a cave and beaten to death with rocks. Koby was my eldest child. He was brilliant and beautiful.

Since then, we have suffered terribly; yet with a lot of help, my husband and my family have been able not only to survive, but to flourish. We created the Koby Mandell Foundation whose flagship program is a therapeutic sleepaway summer camp for bereaved children. Over six thousand children have benefited from Camp Koby in the last fourteen years, including our own children who attended the camp and later served as counselors. The foundation conducts many other programs including psychodrama, ceramics, yoga, and spiritual healing workshops for bereaved mothers. I wrote a prize-winning memoir, *The Blessing of a Broken Heart*, which was translated into three languages and adapted as a stage play. I recently organized a group of bereaved Israeli mothers to speak in the Knesset against the release of Palestinian prisoners. My husband I have lectured around the world. Koby's death mobilized us to become leaders. In our transformation from mourners to activists, my husband and I have learned the art of Jewish resilience.

This book is designed to help you discover resilience in times of sorrow. Although the focus is on bereavement, the book will be helpful for anybody who has suffered a trauma. You may be struggling through a difficult divorce, coping with illness, or nurturing a child who has a disability. Because of my experience, because I've struggled to find resilience for the last thirteen years, clawing and elbowing and climbing my way out of the pit of despair and sadness, I think my experience will be useful to you. I've read much of the literature, spoken to experts. I also spent years training to become a pastoral counselor, a chaplain, after Koby's death because I wanted to understand how to help myself, my family, and others recover from suffering. I counseled and met with hundreds of bereaved people: mothers and fathers and siblings, as well as children who had lost their parents. I worked with cancer patients in the hospital as well as with families whose loved ones had been injured in accidents or suffered terrible illnesses and were now in vegetative states. Along the way I witnessed compelling stories of the power and potency of resilience.

Many people misunderstand the concept of resilience. The literal meaning of the word resilience (from the Latin *resilire*) is to jump or leap back. In other words, to return to who you were, to bounce back. In Hebrew, a word used to denote resilience (*ḥosen*) has the additional meaning of being immunized – in other words, strong and impenetrable. But despite the connotations of the Hebrew word, the Jewish concept of resilience does not mean being impermeable. Nor does it mean to bounce back.

I've attended resilience seminars where psychologists speak about characteristics that enhance resilience like realistic optimism, flexible and curious thinking, empathic emotions, and a problem-solving orientation. They talk about a resilient mindset, the ability to overcome adversity.

But in Jewish thought, resilience isn't an attitude but a process. It's not just endurance or perseverance or stamina, the ability to stand strong and firm. Jewish philosophy teaches us that resilience is not overcoming. It's *becoming*. Becoming more, becoming our fullest and deepest selves as a result of adversity. We don't escape but contemplate and reshape. We don't leap over troubles as if they don't exist. We allow them to be our teachers. *We experience resilience when we are enlarged rather than diminished by our challenges, when facing adversity causes us to change, grow, and become greater.* Moreover, resilience offers us the opportunity to deepen our relationship with the Divine.

You will learn that mourning, the active process of struggling with and transforming the deprivation and grief and sorrow of loss, can motivate and transport you toward a more meaningful and even exalted life. What is most painful can also become an instrument of healing. "The stone the builders rejected has become the cornerstone," states the Psalmist (Ps. 118:22). The stone refers to the Jewish people, who have periodically been ostracized, victimized, and despised. But that which threatened to undermine us – to shatter and destroy – can become the foundation of an enhanced wisdom, appreciation, and joy, the cornerstone of life. Psychologists call this process post-traumatic growth. The Kabbala refers to it as an expanded mind (*moḥin de-gadlut*). In theology, we can call it a sacred ascent.

This book is a primer on Jewish spiritual resilience, the steps you need to traverse in order to face your suffering and be enlarged. We will navigate the spiritual stages of resilience, what I call the seven C's: *chaos, community, choice, creativity, commemoration, consecration,* and *celebration.*

These stages aren't all distinct and you don't have to experience them all or in the order given in this book. The stages are a guide rather than a prescription, a framework for growing from struggle. In striving toward resilience, you will, of course, rise and fall. You will continually renegotiate resilience, relearning this lifelong process.

By entering the chaos and creating from your pain, you will find that doubt, pain, and brokenness will mold your character so that you are more compassionate and live in an enlarged context. You will discover a more authentic self who forms deeper connections to others. Your process of healing may in fact exalt you and propel you toward a more intimate relationship with the Infinite and the Eternal, names that describe God.

ACKNOWLEDGMENTS

I could never have written this book without the support and love of many people. Thank you to those who are so close to our family, especially Valerie Seidner, Roochie Kohlenberg, Yael and Amichai Solomon, Shira and Jonathan Chernoble, Gila and Menachem Weinberg, Anne Seham and Raphael Ruderman, and the "'hood": Gillian and Matanya Freund, Ralph and Michelle Bieber, Shelly and Jeff Alon, and Chanan and Geula Elias. Thank you to our family: Lillian Mandell, Loren and Richard Fogelson, Nancy Lederman, Marilyn and Richard Mandell, Marcy and Larry Mandell, and our nieces and nephews. Thanks to the staff of the Koby Mandell Foundation, especially Roy Angstreich, Jackie Goldman, Moshe Arens, Ami Chaziz, Asher Cohen, Rabbi Gil El Maale, and Aviva Infeld. Special thanks to all of our counselors and head counselors. I can't name you all but it's because of your devotion that Camp Koby can help so many bereaved children and families. Thanks to the staff of the women's healing programs: Tzippi Cedar, Hadassah Ne'eman, Nomi Roth Elbert, Hadassah Cooper, Michelle Gordon, and Zahava Gilmore. And to all of the bereaved mothers we work with and from whom I have learned so much.

Thanks to Todd Salovey for adapting and directing the play, *The Blessing of a Broken Heart*. Thanks to the members of the KMF board past and present: Marla Lerner Tanenbaum, Melodie and Marty Scharf, Margery and Barry Liben, Lee and Cheryl Lasher, Eve and Heshy Feldman, and Todd and Amy Sukol. Thanks to Dina and Jeremy Wimpfheimer and especially Avi Liberman for the gift of Comedy for Koby. Thanks to John and Jane Medved, Steve and Andrea Peskoff, Arlene Ruby, Ruth Mason and Bob Trachtenberg, Dana Ernstoff, Reuven and Joyce Tradburks, Boaz Columbus, Dovid Kupinsky, Anne Breslov, Leah and Alan Lurie, Leah Malamet, Diane Liff, Zahara

Davidowitz, Malka Petrokovsky, Tanya Neppe, Yael Amiel, Mira Cohen, Rena and Ezra Ish Ran, Rochelle Edelson, Sara Eisen, Julie Levine, Batya and Mottle Woolf, Avi and Ruthie Wallfish, Geri Freund, the NAJC, the New York Federation, Shimon Pepper, and Connie and Gary Bachman.

I want to especially thank Matthew Miller and Gila Fine for the care, attention, and love that they gave to this project. And thanks to my editors: Deena Nataf, Charlie Wollman, Tomi Mager, and, most of all, to Shira Koppel.

Love and gratitude to my husband – my partner and teacher in resilience – and to my beloved children: Daniel and Gavi Mandell, Eliana and Avraham Braner. You fill my life with joy. I am so proud of you.

In memory of our parents, Paul and Marilyn Lederman and Jack Mandell.

In memory of Yosef Ish Ran and our dear friend, Shimon Seidner.

In memory of our beloved son Koby Mandell. We miss you every day.

For more information and to be in touch:
sherrimandell@gmail.com
www.kobymandell.org
@mandellsherri (Twitter)

Sherri Mandell
Summer 2015/5775

Chapter One

Chaos   ·

"All that God desires from a person is his heart."
Sanhedrin 106b

Grief at first feels like a state of chaos. Chaos, derived from the Greek word *khaos*, a gaping void, is a state of confusion, of being lost, without control. Once, in the pre-cell phone, pre-GPS era, I was driving with my four small children in upstate New York, and the directions to my friend's home, which included the phone number, literally flew out the open window.

In the chaos of grief, you too may feel that your map has flown out the window. But it's not just that you have no map: you are navigating dark and threatening terrain. You are lost, wandering, unable to see a way out or through or beyond. Your world has crumbled. The anguished encounter with chaos may cause you to despair and lose hope.

Poet Edward Hirsch says that "grief is like an invisible bag of cement that everybody is carrying on their shoulders."

All of us are one day stunned by the weight of loss and pain and despair. And understandably, most of us would like to flee from the chaos that accompanies trauma and bereavement. But allowing uncertainty and darkness may well be the first step toward resilience.

In this chapter, we will learn that when we permit ourselves to enter the chaos, to stumble and cry out, to surrender to our defenselessness, we may find that our pain leads us toward greater truth about both our vulnerability and our power in this world. Entering the chaos prepares us to receive a heightened clarity and wisdom as well as to engage in a more intimate relationship with God.

THE CHANGE OF CHANGE

This change in your life changes everything; you cross a line from which you cannot return to who you were. This isn't like painting the living room a different color or swearing that you will start that diet on Monday. This is The Change. The mother of all change.

You have suffered a change that alters the very system that you live by. No wonder you feel like your world is in chaos. You can't cope or figure life out anymore. You don't believe that anybody can help you, or even understand you.

Consider this, from an opinion piece written by a widow, which appeared in the *New York Times*:

> One of the best pieces of advice I had came from a friend whose husband died suddenly. "Don't forget that you are you," she said cryptically. How right she was. She meant that I should not allow myself to be changed by my experience of grief.

I understand that this woman wants to hold on to her identity. Yet it is foolish to imagine that she would not be changed by grief.

When I graduated from high school, friends wrote in my yearbook: "Don't ever change." Might I have written that to others? Did I mean that we should stay the way we were when we were seniors in high school?

The only way to absorb catastrophe is to expect to change. Think of it, there are so many people who are in therapy, begging for change. So many people chase gurus or hike the Himalayas because they want change. Many seek charismatic teachers because they want to be transformed, renewed, healed.

Unfortunately, it's difficult for people to make positive changes in their life, especially in a way that lasts. Rabbi Israel Salanter, a nineteenth-century rabbi who was the leader of a Lithuanian yeshiva, said that it is harder to change one weak character trait than to learn all sixty-three tractates of the Talmud. Rabbi Salanter stressed that a person had to work on becoming a more ethical, caring person. And that work is very difficult to accomplish because most of us resist internalizing and integrating change. But you have the opportunity to grow. Not just the opportunity. The obligation. And not just the obligation. The necessity.

So know this: resilience entails change. You're not going to bounce back to who you were. Because of your encounter with loss, you are going to bounce forward to become someone you are not yet acquainted with.

ASTONISHMENT

Chaos defines the beginning of all change and creation. The Torah tells us that the world was created from a state of chaos:

"In the beginning of God's creating the heavens and the earth. And the earth was desolate and void, with darkness upon the surface of the deep – and a breath of God hovered over the surface of the waters" (Gen. 1:1–2).

The creation story describes a world of *tohu* and *vohu*, desolation and void, emptiness. The world is engulfed in darkness, its surface covered with waters. There is no firm ground to stand on. You may be able to imagine what this feels like, because it reminds you of the shattering sense of anxiety and emptiness you experience when a person you love has died.

Surprisingly, the Hebrew word for this chaos of desolation and confusion, *tohu*, also conveys wonder. Rashi tells us that *tohu* is astonishment at the presence of emptiness: "For a person would be astonished and amazed at the void in it [the world]." In Rashi's reading, the hypothetical observer perceives that what he now sees as molded and distinct was once without form or definition. What is might not have been. Instead of the something, there might have been nothing: no world, no nature, no stars and planets, no humanity, no magnificence. We contemplate a profound turbulent emptiness in the heart of the world. But instead of leading a person to despair, that intimate knowledge of contingency can spark a profound recognition of wonder.

Of course, when we are confronted with loss, it's rare to believe in any wonder. In fact, disaster may threaten our sanity. I feared that I would not be able to bear the fracture of loss, that I would go mad. Losing Koby was a piercing pain that has lasted for years and will accompany me, in some form, for the rest of my days. And it wasn't just missing my son and the cruelty of his death that toppled my equilibrium. It was also the fact that the world seemed murky and unpredictable and evil. Returning to life seemed as unlikely as standing on water.

The Talmud tells a story of men who journey to an island where they cook and share a meal (Bava Batra 73b). They are shocked when the ground below them begins to tremble. What they think is solid earth is instead a giant sea animal on which sand and grass have grown. When the huge fish suddenly flips over, the men are flung into the sea. If their ship had not been nearby, they surely would have drowned. Their footing is revealed to be shaky, temporary, turbulent.

When we are thrust into the desolation of chaos, we wonder how we will cope and survive. Even the word cope seems meager. We struggle. We wrestle with our pain. One bereaved mother described her experience as an earthquake. Another told me that she felt that her ego had been totally shattered. Booted from our habitual modes of comprehension and our routines, forced to find balance, we may feel totally unequipped to confront our new reality. We are alone, unsteady, trembling; the world may feel capricious, menacing, evil, and our sufferings feel arbitrary.

Yet, if you can allow the chaos, if you can bear the anxiety (often with the help of others), it may be the precursor to the shaping of a new self. While it may feel that your very being is dissolving, you may be undergoing a kind of alchemy, a transmutation of self that will one day invite and include the marvelous.

I am not saying that we should not argue with God, cry out, and plead with Him. Of course, we want only good things in our lives. And we don't want to grow as a result of anguish. The whole notion can seem cruel, almost sadistic. I would prefer to be a more relaxed superficial person with my son alive than be imbued with a profound sense of mission.

But in this suffering there is divinity. When we are in pain, we may not recognize God's presence. But even in the shock, confusion, emptiness, and desolation, God's spirit or *ruaḥ* hovers above us. Rashi compares this action to the hovering of a dove over its nest in a promise of protection. God hovers; He does not force Himself on us. But He does not abandon us.

SOMETHING FROM NOTHING

Psalm 126 is a psalm of hope that, in its final lines, recognizes the deep connection between emptiness and formation:

> They who sow in tears will reap in song.
>> Though he who bears the measure of seed goes on his way weeping,
>> He shall surely come home with exultation, bearing his sheaves.

When it feels that the earth that supported you has been irreparably overturned, there is a promise that new seedlings will one day take root and grow. We are promised a harvest when it seems improbable, when we cannot imagine growth. And this bounty stems from an act of sowing, which is seemingly a more random process than planting. When we plant, we take a seed or seedling and carefully, even gently place it in the ground. If it's a seedling, it's visible. We plant in orderly rows. We know what will most likely grow – the shape, the taste, the texture. We know what to expect.

When we sow, on the other hand, we scatter seeds into the dark ground. If you haven't sown that seed, you probably don't even know that it's there. You haven't put a marker in, written, for example, "green beans" and the date. You can't witness the early signs of growth. Sowing is a process of faith.

Regardless of the means of planting though, every seed has to disintegrate before it can grow into a fruit or vegetable.

Every seed has to break apart to sprout; it has to surrender to the darkness of mystery in order to emerge. That process can feel excruciating. But it is only when the seed turns to nothing that it can, in fact, become something.

Let me repeat that because it is such a stunning truth: *The seed has to turn to nothing to become something.*

How do we cope with the fear and pain of nothingness? By realizing that a crucial aspect of resilience is the ability to allow the darkness, to surrender, to pause there, to suspend our routine, to wait, to receive. We have to stop and allow the waves of pain. We sit and we question and we reflect and we cry. We dwell in a crucible of doubt and imbalance, emptiness, anguish. We are shocked into silence, as if we have returned to the watery depths of creation, before language.

Every birth includes this descent into the mystery of darkness. There are secrets that can be revealed only in the darkness. Those moments of obscurity, rupture, and incomprehensibility are the hallmark of bereavement, grief, mourning, and trauma.

A person who suffers may have to submerge in the anxiety of nothingness. If you don't enter the darkness, you may well never emerge. Poet Donald Hall terms a winter without snow in New England a psychic disaster: "The earth can't emerge because it never submerged." One has to undergo a process of decomposition in order to be reborn.

But how do we do so? What gives us the courage to confront the turmoil and emptiness? Psalm 121 may offer us an answer: "I lift my eyes to the hills, from where will my help come." From where (*me'ayin*) in Hebrew can also mean "from the nothing." Help will come from the chaos itself, from our consciousness of the nothing, of the void and abyss. In trauma, our psyche collides with non-being and discovers that it can tolerate the desolation. Moreover, as we dwell in the darkness we learn that we can see, in the same way that we may see forms and shapes and color even when our eyes are closed. In the nothingness, there is a glimmer of something.

To be able to contain this truth requires deep humility and faith, surrender. It's almost impossible to believe that at the moment of dissolution, rebirth is actually beginning. Yet, it is said that on Tisha B'Av, the darkest day of the Jewish calendar, which marks the catastrophes that have befallen the Jewish people, the Messiah will be born.

We can't see the beginnings of growth: germination is an invisible, mysterious process. And according to the Talmud, "A blessing is present only in something that is hidden from view" (Taanit 8a). Concealment is the first stage in receiving blessing.

The Hebrew word for blessing offers us insight into this promise of rejuvenation. The word blessing, *berakha*, is related to *havrakha*, the agricultural term for the process that describes the rebirth of a grape vine. The vine must submerge, buried in the earth in order to re-emerge. Similarly, where it feels like we have been relegated to darkness, there is growth, fragile new roots forming.

You may feel that God and goodness are concealed from you. But there is blessing there waiting to be discovered, to be revealed. First one has to encounter the chaos, allow the pain and desolation to penetrate one's being.

STUMBLING

Everybody will tell you to be strong. But the key, as far as I have seen, is to give yourself permission to be soft and vulnerable – to allow yourself to stumble. It sounds simple but many people would rather just skip this step and stand strong. If I counted how many times people told me to "BE STRONG," I think I would get to over a thousand. But one young man told me,

"Guard your strength." I think that advice was much more helpful.

Vulnerability is also a strength that we need to protect. Admitting vulnerability is not something we are taught or something that is valued. The source of the word *vulnerable* is the Latin word for wound. Being vulnerable means that we may reveal our wounds and our doubts and our fears. Most of us are not comfortable admitting fear or pain. Instead, we think we are supposed to be perfect, confident, strong, sure of ourselves. And when we aren't, not all of those around us can receive or appreciate our expressions of uncertainty. Yet vulnerability may be our deepest form of power. We have to choose when and where we express it.

As a speaker, I have learned the power of vulnerability. I lecture frequently about my book *The Blessing of a Broken Heart* as well as about the work of the Koby Mandell Foundation. I used to be afraid to speak because I feared making a mistake. But now, when I lecture, I know it's okay to be imperfect. If I forget where my speech was leading, what my next story was going to be, I ask the audience what my last point was. Everybody in the room seems to relax. I do as well. When I give myself permission to be vulnerable, the lecture is more honest, more immediate, more powerful – and the connection with the audience more potent.

Dennis Regan, a comedian who has appeared on *The Tonight Show with Jay Leno* and in films, told me that some of the biggest laughs he gets are when he makes a mistake and flubs a joke, because the audience relates to him and feels empathy for him.

The Talmud teaches that one should be soft like a reed, not hard like a cedar (Taanit 20a). A reed bends beneath the storm without breaking. Flexible yet firm, the humble reed is privileged to be fashioned into an instrument for writing Torah scrolls, participating in holiness.

The reed teaches us that the ability to bend and surrender can lead us toward a more holy relationship with the world. When we relinquish our defenses, our usual postures, our habitual stance toward life, we may discover enhanced intimacy with others and with the Divine. Rabbi Isaac Hutner, a twentieth-century American *rosh yeshiva* and rabbi, cites the rabbinic aphorism, "One never gets the true sense of [literally, stands upon] the words of Torah until one has mistaken them [literally, stumbled over them]" (Gittin 43a).

When we stumble, we encounter the world and the words anew. Pushed out of our conditioned responses, we grapple with meaning. When we lose our stability, when we falter, we grope toward a tenuous but perhaps more authentic and vital standing, as we struggle to find our footing. Because we can no longer rely on habit or conditioning, we may experience truths about ourselves, about those around us, and about the Divine that were previously inaccessible.

Instead of being resentful and angry and bitter about the injustice or indignity of what we have to endure, we may discover that our vulnerability creates a more honest and urgent relationship with others and with God.

THE POWER IN VULNERABILITY

In Jewish texts, the Messiah, the redeemer who will bring peace to the world, is not described as a hero, but rather as a vulnerable person. In the archetypal Jewish story of healing, the Messiah is a wounded beggar waiting with the other beggars at the gates of the city:

> R. Joshua ben Levi came upon Elijah the prophet while he was standing at the entrance of R. Shimon ben Yoḥai's cave. He asked Elijah, "When will the Messiah come?"

"Go and ask him yourself," he said.
"Where is he?"
"Sitting at the gates of the city."
"How shall I know him?"
"He is sitting among the poor covered with wounds. The others unbind all their wounds at the same time and then bind them all up again. But he unbinds them one at a time and then binds it up again, saying to himself: 'Perhaps I shall be needed. If so, I must always be ready so as not to delay for a moment.'" (Sanhedrin 98a)

The Messiah in this passage is not a warrior, but rather a vulnerable, wounded healer who can feel others' pain. Unlike the other beggars, he is able to rise from his own pain to give from the place of brokenness. What distinguishes him, I think, is his responsiveness and alacrity. He sits at the gate, the portal to the city, wrapping his wounds one by one so he can leap when called.

It may be agonizing to touch our wounds or to be present when somebody else is suffering. Most of us don't want to sit at the gates with the beggars applying bandages on oozing sores. We want to stay as far away from others who suffer as we can.

Pain threatens to unravel us. But remarkably, it is sometimes our wounds that bestow authority. In the Torah, Jacob struggles all night with a mysterious angel who wounds him in his hip socket, causing him to limp for the rest of his life. Yet the angel cannot vanquish him. Moreover, Jacob asks for and receives a blessing from the angel (Gen. 32:27–30). His name is changed from Jacob to Israel – he who struggles with man and the Divine and prevails. From then on, he is called by both of his names. In this way, God assures us that although we may be wounded and limping, eventually, our greatest struggles can also become the source of blessings. We do not have to distract ourselves from our damaged places. Instead our struggles can become sources of vitality.

CALLING OUT

The Torah recognizes that there is a potent connection between defenselessness and a person's need to pray. In Hebrew the word for vulnerability (*pegiut*) is derived from the words for a blow or injury – but its less common meaning denotes prayer. When Jacob flees from his brother Esau who is intent on murdering him, he leaves his family in Beersheva and journeys alone to Harran. The text tells us that he encounters (*vayifga*) "the place" and spends the night there (Gen. 28:11). Rabbi Samson Raphael Hirsch translates the language of encounter, *vayifga*, as meaning that Jacob was struck by the place, a collision. Rashi, quoting the sages, tells us that the word *vayifga* also means "to pray." Indeed, this encounter is regarded as the source of the daily evening prayer, that of the darkness when we are most fearful and it is hardest to see God's loving hand. When we collide with our own vulnerability, we may be urged toward the language of prayer. We cry out in our raw need.

So many people will tell you not to cry. But crying doesn't mean that you will break apart. On the contrary, it is the first, most essential step in mourning, in finding your elemental voice, in mending yourself.

Please understand that being brokenhearted does not mean being depressed. Depression is a black hole, a vortex that seizes us with a power from which we can't escape, a molecular sadness. But being broken is, in a way, the human condition. All of us will be broken at one stage or another.

We cry out because ordinary language cannot express the *tohu* and *vohu* of our experience, the chaos of our great desolation. That primal cry, the inarticulate language of confusion and despair and hopelessness, describes the shocking encounter with the pain of the void, the despair at the seeming emptiness. In this cataclysmic reality, we call out for help, for our pain to lessen, for understanding, for connection to another world because only God can comfort us. But our cry is also necessary in order to arouse God's compassion.

In the Torah, it is only when God hears the Hebrew people crying out from their suffering as slaves in Egypt that He speaks to Moses and tells him that He sees and hears their suffering – He *knows* of their experience of pain – and will remember them and bring them out of their slavery. It is the people's cry that initiates the Exodus from Egypt, the return to Israel: the redemption (Ex. 3). God requires that we call to Him; and then He responds to our outcry.

CLOSURE AND DISCLOSURE

In the Torah portion of *Lekh Lekha*, God tells Abraham to leave his country, his birthplace, and the house of his parents, and journey to the land which God will show him. He has to leave behind everything he knows in order to discover his new identity and his connection to God. Vulnerable, he has to wander, to wait for signs.

Lekh Lekha means "go for yourself." The chaos may well be the first step on your path of reshaping yourself. In our vulnerability and brokenness, God calls on us to go for ourselves. It can be scary to be dislocated, disorienting to abandon our past comforts and identity, but, as a result of becoming wanderers, we may find that we discover wonder in the world.

For trauma can be followed by disclosure. At Mount Sinai, when God speaks to the Hebrew people, a midrash tells us, their souls fly from them, but then the people experience a

sense of rebirth. After the smoke, the lightning, and the shofar blasts comes the giving of the Ten Commandments. The
people's terror of annihilation is followed by revelation, state-
ments of divine truth.

And something parallel may happen in our personal lives
when we are struck by cataclysm. The trembling can be followed by insight, knowledge, and divine gifts. That revelation
can come as a feeling of love or communion with everybody
else who is suffering, a sense of purpose, or even acceptance
of one's situation. It may be an understanding of the limits of
this world, or a desire for contact with the World to Come, a
longing to peek through the flimsy curtain separating worlds.
It can be a greater belief in God or a greater compassion and
generosity toward others.

What we most want to shirk, to change, to abandon, can
be the centerpiece of blossoming that separates us from who
we were, and transports us to a place where we can more fully
realize our greater selves.

Therefore, it is a problem to think of closure as the goal
of any grieving process. Most people understandably want to
close the door on their pain. They want to finish with it. They
want to return to the life that they had before. The word "closure" is mentioned almost immediately in the news broadcasts
after any tragedy, after any grief. But closure is a fallacy. While
we don't want the pain, it's important to understand that there
is *disclosure* hiding there, something that waits to be revealed.

BEYOND THE DESOLATION

That is not to say that we invite suffering into our lives. In fact,
Judaism teaches that we should not remain in the chaos of
pain, and we should help others to exit this unbearable and
dangerous territory. We can think of the chaos as being similar

to the top 848 meters of Mount Everest, known as the "Death Zone." There, climbers can rely on only 30 percent of the oxygen found at sea level. They often become confused, and may find it difficult to sleep and eat. Their digestion slows. Wounds cannot heal. If a person stays there too long, he or she can lose consciousness or die.

Jewish law recognizes that the days following a loved one's death are fraught with chaos. The bereaved are in a state of psychological frailty. For that reason, the bereaved have a different status of *aninut* until after the burial. They are not obligated to pray or perform other commandments because they are in turmoil; the chaos of death and pain threatens and topples their composure.

If a person remains in this unprotected territory of raw pain and need indefinitely, he or she won't be able to heal. On the other hand, if a person doesn't allow the trauma entrance, she or he may never recover.

Think of entering your suffering as being similar to diving. When I snorkel in the Red Sea, I am shocked by the brilliant colors of the schools of iridescent fish and formations of coral that are invisible from the surface. You may lose your bearings, you may fear that you are going to drown, but after the fear and trauma, know that, in the darkness, you will encounter sparks of beauty.

QUESTIONS:

- What did you learn about chaos as a child? In your home? In your school? In your community? In your own life?
- What does chaos say to you? Write one sentence that chaos seems to whisper to you.
- What can you respond to chaos? Write a sentence responding to chaos.
- Write about a time that you stumbled. What happened? Who helped you?
- What does it mean to you to be vulnerable?
- What is the difference for you between closure and disclosure?
- To whom can you cry out?
- How did your family of origin deal with grief?
- What did you learn about grief as a child? What did you learn in your school or community? What did you learn about it as an adult?
- What is your personal prayer for healing?

Chapter Two

Community

"The world is built with acts of kindness."

Psalms 89:3

In Jewish thought, creating resilience rests not only on the individual but on the community. Most of our prayers are in the plural. We do not praise the rugged individual who cares only for himself. Instead, the individual is judged on his willingness to give to others, to protect the weak. More than a network or a neighborhood or an organization, community is a profound feeling of responsibility for others, a compassion that allows us to share a sense of mission and destiny in healing the world.

Right now, you probably need to receive kindness from others. Eventually you will be able to give in greater, fuller kindness, because your knowledge of compassion has been enhanced. You will feel a greater sense of community, a profound sense of connection to others that offers you resilience.

THE PRISONER CANNOT FREE HIMSELF

Kindness can break through the boundaries between us, the isolation. When a person suffers, it can feel like solitary confinement, as if he or she were in prison. One summer at Camp Koby, the therapeutic sleepaway camp our foundation runs for four hundred bereaved children, that feeling of imprisonment was demonstrated when an art therapist asked the junior high school kids to draw comics, dividing the bereaved teenagers into groups. The kids were told to make up stories about a hero, drawing pictures and then writing captions about each hero's journey.

After the session was over, the large poster papers with their colorful drawings were still hanging on the wall. When my husband and I entered the room and asked the therapist how he thought the session had gone, he seemed skeptical. But when my husband looked at the cartoons, he realized that every single one had a prison scene, with somebody behind bars, or with their wrists tied in handcuffs, or trying to escape.

In order to overcome the isolation of suffering, we need the presence of someone who cares. No matter how strong a person's intellectual or spiritual beliefs, the experience of sorrow threatens one's equilibrium and sometimes one's sanity. Even the greatest talmudic rabbis, who had tremendous faith in God and in the ultimate purifying power of pain, could not bear their suffering alone. When R. Ḥanina visited R. Yoḥanan, who was ill, he asked him, "Are these sufferings welcome to you?" R. Yoḥanan answered, "Neither they nor their reward." R. Ḥanina saw that R. Yoḥanan was in pain and said, "Give me your hand." R. Yoḥanan reached out his hand and R. Ḥanina raised him up. Our sages ask, "Why could R. Yoḥanan not raise himself?" The text answers, "The prisoner cannot free himself from jail" (Berakhot 5b).

No matter how strong our faith, when suffering strikes, we need others to help us unlock the prison of our suffering. Furthermore, when people join together, pain is lessened. The Talmud states that when one visits the sick, the visitor takes away one sixtieth of the patient's pain (Nedarim 39b). A study on friendship conducted at the University of Virginia confirms a similar phenomenon. When two friends climb a hill together, the hill seems less steep than when they climb it alone. In addition, the longer the pair have known each other, the easier the climb appears.

Martin Buber quotes the hasidic masters: "When a man is singing and cannot lift his voice, and another comes and sings with him, another who can lift his voice, the first will be able to lift his voice too. That is the secret of the bond between spirits."

TIME DOESN'T HEAL — BUT KINDNESS CAN

Most people aren't aware of how crucial a role the community plays in protecting its members from the damage associated with trauma. It's not only how we react to what happens to us, but how the community receives and shelters us afterwards that defines our ability to heal. Recent studies have noted that the extent of a victim's trauma may to a large degree rest on how he or she is nurtured by the community. In a study of 141 former child soldiers in Nepal (between the ages of five and fourteen years old), Dr. Brandon Kohrt, a global mental health expert and assistant professor at Duke University, found that the children's postwar mental health was more dependent on how their families and villages welcomed, received, and supported them than on what atrocities the fighters had witnessed or experienced. American soldiers returning from the wars in Iraq and Afghanistan report a similar phenomenon. It may well be the support of the community that defines our mental health.

Trauma and sorrow are too much of a burden for a family to carry by itself. I know that my family might well have collapsed if we had been left on our own after my son's murder. On the first night after Koby was killed, when I went upstairs to my room, resting on my pillow was a little bunch of wildflowers from a friend, with a card. Just when I thought I would die, I smiled. Because my friend had entered my room to give me love. When my husband decided to go to America to speak five weeks after my son's death, a sixteen-year-old girl from our community, Aviva, moved in with us. Neighbors continually brought us food and visited. Women from Efrat brought us Shabbat meals for well over six months. We felt supported, cradled, and embraced by the community.

During the summer of 2012, Lia, a thirteen-year-old girl, attended Camp Koby. Lia's father was murdered during the second intifada by Arabs who worked with him at an industrial complex.

The first day of camp, Lia's counselor, Ronit, noticed Lia scratching at something under her watch. Later, when Ronit asked about it, the girl told her that she had been cutting herself. The camp therapist and the director spoke to Lia's mother, who asked us to keep her at camp. The staff agreed to keep close watch on her. By the end of the camp, when the counselor and Lia were getting on the bus home, Lia unstrapped her watch and showed Ronit that her wounds had disappeared. "Time doesn't heal," she said. "Love does." She hugged her counselor.

Loving-kindness can indeed heal. At Camp Koby, we do a lot of hugging. We also have art and drama and nature and animal therapies. Last summer, one of our campers, a ten-year-old girl, Ma'ayan, whose father had died of cancer, had a terrible stutter. Her counselors could hardly understand her. By the end of camp, Ma'ayan had lost her stutter. When she returned home, her mother couldn't believe it, but her daughter could now speak freely.

KINDNESS AND RESPONSIBILITY

According to Jewish mysticism, God created the world so that He could bestow loving-kindness to His creation. If He were alone, there would be no one to receive the gift of creation.

We are made in God's image and God's primary impulse is kindness. Therefore when we are kind, we act in the way of God. In practicing compassion and kindness, we come close to our most godly selves.

In addition, kindness allows us to practice justice. *Tzedaka*, charity, is derived from the word for justice. When the world isn't fair, people can step in to redress injustice, to give to others. Thus, the rabbis of the Talmud criticize a person who only studies and doesn't perform acts of kindness. And a midrash tells us that the stork is not considered a kosher animal because it cares only for its own.

The injunction to be kind is so paramount that we are not only supposed to sympathize with another person's pain but also to share in his or her distress as if it were our own suffering. We can learn this from the Torah's description of Moshe's actions while the Children of Israel battled Amalek:

> But Moses's hands were heavy; and they took a stone and put it under him, and he sat upon it. The rabbis of the Talmud wondered, did Moses not have a cushion or a bolster to sit on? Rather, they answered, this is what Moses meant to convey: "As Israel is in distress I too will share with them. And whoever shares in the distress of the community will merit to behold its consolation." (Taanit 11a)

Feeling the pain of others can mobilize us to take initiative to alleviate it. Perhaps God chose Moses as a leader because, from the outset, he assumed responsibility for easing the suffering of other people. One of his first daring (and shocking) acts as a young man was to murder an Egyptian who was beating a Hebrew slave. He not only shared the pain of others, but acted to relieve it.

It's significant that, in kabbalistic terms, another Hebrew word for kindness is *gedula*, which generally denotes greatness. As we expand our sense of self to serve others, we become more resilient people because we are less isolated and more interwoven with a community – more generous in spirit. You may find that with time you become emotionally larger, more available, and a more compassionate and sensitive person. You change your center of gravity, extend your borders – your boundaries – to come closer to other people.

In fact, the ability to give and receive kindness may be the way that we best express our humanity. Rabbi Eliyahu Dessler, in his book *Mikhtav MeEliyahu*, says that what is most difficult for a prisoner in isolation is not the loneliness so much as the fact that he is unable to give. According to psychoanalyst Erich Fromm, a person's deepest need is the need to overcome separateness, to leave the prison of one's aloneness.

THE SOURCE OF KINDNESS

What is it about giving and kindness that is so crucial? It's not just that "as you give so shall you receive," a reciprocal relationship of getting back as a result of giving. Rather, giving is sacred because in order to perform kindness, we truly come closer to God. We must contract ourselves and our own preoccupations in a way that is similar to *tzimtzum*, the mystical doctrine of divine contraction as a pre-condition to the creation of the

world. Psychologist James Hillman says that "God had to create by withdrawal: he created the not-him, the other, by self-
concentration.... On the human level, withdrawal of myself aids
the other to come into being." As God had to absent Himself
in order to make a place available for humans, we, similarly,
surrender our own preoccupations in order to serve others. We
participate in a greater good, fostering a feeling of unity with
others and the Divine. In so doing, our identity is not erased
or diminished but enlarged. We relieve the isolation of suffering. We break the brittle boundaries that divide us.

One might assume that the ability to relinquish one's
own preoccupations stems from a person's strong sense of
security and feeling of wholeness. Yet in his book *The Wounded
Healer*, Christian theologian Henri Nouwen states that a person
who is a healing presence recognizes his own brokenness and
loneliness – the depths of the human condition. As a result,
he has the courage to deepen another person's pain so that it
can be shared. Then the pain does not paralyze and isolate but
mobilizes a liberating sense of hope, spurred by a shared sense
of the loneliness and brokenness of being human. A community is formed.

I believe that the biblical figure Abraham models an additional and important aspect of kindness. His story also begins
with a stripping away of self. After all, this is the man who left
his homeland and his family in order to find himself, and to
find God. Yet the emphasis in this paradigm of giving is on faith
in God's plenty. Rather than sharing loneliness and brokenness,
we affirm and transmit bounty, the unlimited goodness that
we intuit in our relationship with the Divine. Our giving is an
offering sourced in a belief in divine abundance.

Consider the story in the Torah. On a terribly hot day,
Abraham sits at the entrance to his tent waiting for guests, even

though he is a man of ninety-nine recovering from the circumcision he has performed on himself. With all four sides of the tent open to visitors, he hopes, despite his pain, to offer wayfarers a meal (Gen. 19). The Midrash teaches that God made the day particularly sweltering, to save Abraham the bother of guests, but still Abraham makes himself available, looking for people to feed, to host, to serve. (I'm reminded of the story about the Messiah who also makes himself accessible, sitting at the open gates of the city.) And all this on the third day after the circumcision, the day on which, according to Rashi, the wound is most painful.

Abraham busies himself (and his wife) preparing food for these angels. Yet angels don't eat. Why this absurd situation? The angels provide Abraham the opportunity to give, to act in the divine image. It seems that Abraham does not accept his identity as an ill person. Instead, he sees himself foremost as a man of kindness, a provider. As a result, he is visited by angels and the appearance of God.

The Torah teaches us that when we surrender our own limitations in order to give, we may well engage in the realm of the Divine. By overlooking and overcoming limits and restraints, we experience a mode of transcendence which is unbounded, a connection to the infinite. The generosity that began from a place of brokenness grows into an expansive sense of wholeness, a trust and faith in abundance. Each encounter offers a meeting with the boundless Divine, in ourselves and others.

THE NATURE OF KINDNESS

Yet there are many people who do not want to ask for help, and refuse it when it's given, because they don't want to admit weakness, distress, or need. A bereaved mother I know told me that she would never ask anybody for help because she had to stand on her own feet. Thus, it's not surprising that the word for kindness in Hebrew, *ḥesed*, can also mean disgrace (certain rare words in Hebrew can also mean their opposite, a linguistic phenomenon known as a contronym). Can we allow ourselves to experience the healing power of kindness or do we feel shamed at being its beneficiary?

For others, bestowing kindness may feel unnatural, alien. They are afraid to interfere, to get too close to another person. They worry that they may be overstepping boundaries, that the person who suffers does not want their help. They mind their own business, distance themselves, refuse to enter another's privacy because they see it as an invasion.

Yet it's striking that sometimes after a person has received great kindness, it becomes easier for him or her to give, to risk reaching out to another. Even if such individuals were not the type to be compassionate before, the kindness fills them so much that it overflows. They want to pass it on to others. It's almost as if they intuit what Lewis Hyde writes: "The spirit of a gift is kept alive by its constant donation." The nature of kindness is to be transferred onward.

When something aches, we call it tender. The question is: Can we allow our own tenderness, the places of our wounds, to eventually serve ourselves and others so that we cultivate tenderness, the soft, elastic quality of kindness and love?

LEARNING A NEW LANGUAGE

Some bereaved people turn away from others who could help them because they can't take the chance that somebody will make an insensitive or unkind comment. As a pastoral counselor, I've learned to preface many of my meetings with this sentence: "If I say something hurtful, please tell me and know that I didn't intend to."

Language, intended to facilitate community, often becomes a charged issue when you experience upheaval in your life. You may not be able to bear ordinary language, when people speak about the mundane, when people complain about small annoyances. You will no doubt feel that people say stupid things to you and may be tempted to isolate yourself, which, unfortunately, can lead to more suffering.

It is also difficult for those who have suffered trauma or bereavement to share their own experience, to find the right words, the fitting words, the words that can describe and circumscribe and contain their own struggles. Aharon Appelfeld, an Israeli author, has written many books set during the Holocaust in an attempt to communicate the devastating and complicated knowledge of what he and others endured.

When Appelfeld was eight years old, soldiers shot his mother dead in the yard of their home in Bukovina. Soon after, he and his father were sent to a concentration camp in Transnistria but were separated. Appelfeld escaped from the camp and survived on his own for years, foraging for food in the forest, hiding in barns. Later he lived with peasants in the countryside. It wasn't until Appelfeld was in his twenties that he was reunited with his father in Israel. He hadn't known that his father had survived the war.

In his autobiography, Appelfeld says that he "prefers stuttering, for in stuttering I hear the friction and the disquiet, the effort to purge impurities from the words, the desire to offer something from inside you. Smooth, fluent sentences leave me with a feeling of uncleanness, of order that hides emptiness."

When the Torah says that Moses was heavy of tongue, perhaps it means that because of his experience, he felt discord and disquiet. After all, he had been exiled from his home as a baby, placed in a small basket on the Nile after Pharaoh decreed that all Hebrew baby boys be killed. After he was rescued by Pharaoh's daughter, he was brought up in a palace, separated from his family. He knew the pain of fracture and displacement.

Scientists confirm that when a person suffers a trauma, language itself is damaged. According to Professor David Pelcovitz of Yeshiva University, studies of trauma victims indicate that the language center of the brain, Broca's area, is disturbed, shut down. At first a person in the shock of trauma may need silence. That accords with the *shiva* practice that visitors should not speak until the mourner does. It's almost as if a mourner is thrown back into the primordial reality before the world was created, before language.

But few who try to comfort are able to tolerate that silence. Many people will give advice, they will tell you how long you are allowed to be sad, and what therapist you should go to, and what you should eat, and which tea will ease the burning in your throat. They cannot tolerate the spaces in the conversation, and they fill them with words. In fact, a large part of my training as a pastoral counselor was learning how to be silent, how to be present to listen to another person without interrupting to fill the emptiness.

With time, a significant factor in healing is finding a language to describe and encompass our experience and reconnect us to community. That's why a support group can be so helpful. After experiencing trauma, in many ways, you speak a different language, one that is more pure – fraught with pain but also more sensitive to nuance.

BECOMING A TEACHER

In July 2014, three Israeli boys, Naftali Fraenkel, Gilad Shaer, and Eyal Yifrah, were kidnapped and found murdered eighteen days later near Hebron. The next day, an acquaintance, a doctor whom I encountered at a ceremony celebrating the birth of a baby girl, said to me, "At least those boys were killed in that car right away. They didn't suffer. You know, I think your son suffered more."

I felt as if he had taken his fist and jabbed me in the gut. I was so unguarded, vulnerable. But I said to him, "Do you think telling me that helps me?" The doctor thanked me for telling him how I felt. But I was deeply injured by what he had said. Sometimes it's too painful to share our feelings with others. Or sometimes we may feel that they just won't understand.

A few weeks following Koby's murder, a friend of mine complained to me about having to go to a school meeting for her eighth-grade son who was in Koby's class. I felt so sad, startled, shattered, but I didn't say anything. Later I felt angry with my friend. What I would have done to be able to go to a school meeting for Koby! When I spoke to a grief counselor, she told me: "Sometimes you have to let people know that they have hurt you. You have to become a teacher."

Thinking of any hurt that way allows us to be kind to ourselves – and others. It's not that others are insensitive. It's that they truly don't understand. Instead of feeling hurt or insulted, we may be called upon to educate others to be more sensitive and compassionate. Instead of isolating ourselves, we share the wisdom of our experience. By allowing others to know our emotional selves, we create stronger bonds with them. Of course you can't go around teaching everybody – you would wear yourself out. But if you value a relationship, think of yourself as somebody who has wisdom, insight, and feelings to convey to others. By sharing your inner truths, you strengthen your sense of community with others, as well as their ability to understand. You fortify their emotional intelligence. You help build the compassion of the community.

HOLY WORK

Before the angels visit Abraham in the desert, God appears to him outside of his tent in order to perform the act of visiting the sick, thus establishing a biblical precedent that obliges us to take care of the ill and infirm. Yet Abraham turns away from God to tend to his guests, the three angels. Rashi says that Abraham asks God to wait while he welcomes the wayfarers. From this exchange, we learn the great importance of kindness. It can even preempt a conversation with God.

In the Rashbam's reading of the story, on the other hand, the angels are a manifestation of God, His messengers. Abraham is in essence feeding God. Giving can thus be defined as nurturing the sacred in ourselves and others.

But not everybody understands that kindness can be a form of sacred service. For many years, the Koby Mandell Foundation ran two-day healing retreats for widows or bereaved mothers whose husbands or children were murdered by terrorists. Fifteen to twenty women were taken to a hotel, where they participated in healing programs that included dance and art therapy, support groups, massage, yoga, and walks on the beach. One day, the American ambassador's wife wanted to honor our work by joining us at one of these retreats. I introduced her to Shira Chernoble, a grief counselor and massage therapist and a very good friend of mine. She told Shira, "I really admire you for doing this kind of work. It must be very difficult. So draining and exhausting. I don't know how you do it."

Shira answered her, "For me, it would be more difficult to drive a taxi all day. Or to do telemarketing. But to do this work is an honor. To be with these women in their pain, to me that is a privilege. It's holy work."

It's a privilege to be with people who open up to you in their pain. It's a privilege to find that place of listening and hospitality in your own heart. One who helps the bereaved needs to learn to receive from others so that she is not depleted. But when a person helps others with their pain, together they join in a sacred space of love and caring and truth.

BEING KIND TO YOURSELF

If you blame yourself or others for your problems, you may not be able to recognize kindness even when others offer it to you. You will be wary and defensive.

We can learn from people who refuse to engage in useless blame. I once worked with a physical therapist, the mother of ten children, who was diagnosed with bone cancer when she was in her late forties. Her primary doctor had told her not to worry, that her back pain was normal. She didn't go back to the doctor for a few months, precious time that might have improved her prognosis. Yet she told me that she had decided that she would not blame herself or others. Of course she wished that her doctor had sent her for tests right away. But she was not going to second-guess what had happened. She was not going to live the few years remaining to her in bitterness.

Blame and guilt and shame can certainly erode our resilience. After my son's murder, I told Rabbi Avraham Twersky that I felt guilty because we had brought our son to Israel, to Judea, when we could have stayed in Silver Spring. We had brought him to a dangerous part of the world, and our worst fears had been realized. (When I write political articles, the talkbacks often tell me that I am responsible for my son's murder. Instead of blaming the terrorists, they fault the victim.)

Rabbi Twersky said that eventually we would be able to deal with the grief, but if we allowed ourselves to be overcome with guilt, it would kill us. What I've come to understand in the subsequent years is that in order to overcome guilt, we need to work on forgiving ourselves. And forgiving ourselves begins with love, for ourselves, our family, and for God who created a world that includes suffering. Of course this is the central question of theodicy: Why do good people suffer? When Moses asked to see God's glory, he was told that he could not see God's face but only His back (Ex. 33:20–23). In other words, we can't apprehend divine justice or mercy. We can only look for meaning retrospectively.

But though we can't see God, we can see each other's faces. And it is the love and kindness that we receive from others that can shield us from pain when God seems so distant.

Before Gerda Weissmann Klein's brother, Arthur, went off to war in 1939, she promised him that she would take care of their parents. Germany had invaded Poland and her brother was drafted into the German army. She never saw him again, and her parents were killed during the war, but she entertained the irrational hope that her brother would somehow reappear and reassure her that she had done a good job. Years later, Prime Minister Menachem Begin, who had read her book, approached her and said, "I have waited so long to meet Arthur's little sister."

She cried, and he said, "You have been very brave." Begin uncannily provided the praise she'd been longing for. Somehow, as a result, she felt "balm on that still-festering wound." Begin was able to help heal a wound from the past with a loving gesture, providing the reassurance and comfort she had been seeking for years.

THE LOVING VOICE WITHIN

Those lucky people who had kind parents who cared for them in a nurturing way are often better able to withstand trauma because they have internalized a compassionate voice, a voice of kindness. They have a voice of comfort within themselves. As a result, they are more likely to be able to both give and receive kindness, and allow themselves to be loved by a community.

Insecure parenting produces adults who are more likely to feel hostility or alienation. In a study of Holocaust survivors, Dr. Nancy Isserman found that fifty years after World War II, those survivors who had experienced secure parenting as children defined themselves as less hateful or vengeful than those who had weaker bonds with their parents.

I realize that my parents' unconditional love helped me survive my son's murder because it taught me that I had worth – no matter what. But no matter how you were parented, there are things you can do right now to be kind to yourself, to love yourself. You can't go back and get parents to whom you are more attached, but you can still determine that you will be tender and kind to yourself, insisting on your own worth, no matter what your circumstances.

To do so takes courage, a word derived from the Latin for heart. You may decide to turn to others, to ask for professional help, to join a support group – to find those who can nurture you. You may need to do yoga or swim or run or lift weights in order to free yourself from the pain of loss. You may need to give yourself time, moments or hours to sit and reflect. You may want to study the Psalms, learn Torah. Whatever you need, now is the time to give it to yourself.

CONNECTION AND CONTINUITY

We can expand our definition of community beyond the people who are near to us. Community can also be a connection to people far away or a relationship with our past, to our history, to our heritage, to others who have gone before us and provided wisdom. We are not alone but part of a great chain of people.

When I pray from the prayer book, I sometimes think of all the people before me who have said the same prayers and all the people around me who are still saying the same prayers. And those in the future who will continue to whisper the same words. The prayers provide connection and continuity, a source of resilience.

Ilan Ramon was a hero, not just because he was the first Israeli astronaut, but also because he felt a responsibility to embody a Jewish presence in space in order to represent the community and continuity of the Jewish people. In 2003, during his space voyage on the *Challenger*, he ate special kosher meals and kept Shabbat in space on Cape Kennedy time.

His mother had survived Auschwitz, so it was especially important to him to bring along items of Jewish significance as well as those that memorialized the Holocaust. These included a microfiche of a Torah, an artistic mezuza made from barbed wire, a dollar from the Lubavitcher Rebbe, and a copy of the drawing "Moon Landscape" by Petr Ginz. When Ilan Ramon was preparing for his space voyage, he took a tour of the Yad Vashem art museum, where he saw this drawing of the earth as viewed from the moon. Ginz, a boy from Prague, had drawn the sketch when he was imprisoned in Theresienstadt at the age of fourteen. Two years later, Petr was murdered in Auschwitz.

The *Challenger* crashed on February 1, 2003, on what would have been Petr Ginz's seventy-fifth birthday. While practically everything on the spaceship was burned up, thirty-seven pages of Ilan Ramon's diary were recovered, some of them in Palestine, Texas.

Another diary was found in Prague as a result of that crash: Petr Ginz's diary of the years 1941–1942, before he was deported to Theresienstadt. Following the media attention about the space shuttle, a landlord cleaning up his apartment in Prague after a tenant's departure found Petr's diary and realized he had discovered an important document.

He got in touch with Petr's sister, Chava Pressburger, who now lives in Israel. Sixty years later, Chava read what her brother had written as a boy. The diaries were later published in the Czech Republic and translated into English and other languages. The Czech Republic issued a commemorative stamp that combined the image of the drawing "Moon Landscape" with a photo of Petr Ginz. The diary that Petr Ginz had written in his bedroom in Prague, his observations at the age of fourteen, suddenly leaped over decades and spread to the world.

After I read Petr Ginz's diary, I called Chava Pressburger, and my son Daniel and I drove down to her home in Omer, a town in the south of Israel, to meet her and her husband. We sat in her living room, and she unwrapped two small notebooks as if she were revealing a precious jewel.

In her introduction to the diary, Chava says that when she read Petr's words, after an interval of sixty years, "I felt as if Petr hadn't actually died. It seemed to me that he was alive somewhere in eternity and was letting me know by sending this particular message."

The confluence of a space launch, a drawing of the earth as seen from the moon by a boy who was brutally killed, and his newly discovered diary dramatically highlighted a connection that continued, transcending the barriers of time and space.

Here is another example of the power of extended community.

In 1977, Natan Sharansky, the Soviet dissident, was sentenced to thirteen years in prison as an alleged spy for America. His wife, Avital, who had immigrated to Israel, led a tireless campaign for his release. As a result of international pressure,

Sharansky was released in 1986, after nine years in prison. He came directly to Israel.

In 2006, the Koby Mandell Foundation conducted a special summer camp for children who had been expelled from their homes in Gush Katif the previous summer as a result of the 2005 withdrawal from the Gaza-area settlements. Understandably, these kids were extremely angry at the Israeli government for evicting them forcibly from their homes, upending their sense of stability, their places of residence, their communities, their parents' livelihoods.

Avital Sharansky worked as a psychologist at the camp and Natan came to visit. He spoke to the group of kids and told them about how he had survived prison in the Soviet Union. He was often housed in solitary confinement, but he refused to succumb to his jailers' power. He didn't want to give his captors that pleasure. A chess prodigy, he played games in his head and he also read from a book of Psalms that Avital had given him. And he and the other prisoners found a way to communicate with each other by Morse code, knocking on the walls of each other's cells.

One day in May, the prisoners were aware that it was the Israeli Memorial Day, Yom HaZikaron. They arranged, through tapping in Morse code, to observe a moment of silence together, to mark the deaths of Israeli soldiers. You can imagine the power of that moment. Isolated in a Soviet prison, they managed to transcend their misery and torment to forge a connection to the Jewish people and Jewish history. Years later, Sharansky was present at the official Memorial Day ceremonies on Mount Herzl in Jerusalem as a minister in the Israeli government. But, he told us, observing the day in prison had been his most significant and meaningful Memorial Day.

When one of the Camp Koby kids asked him how he had managed to survive the *gulag* under such terrible conditions, he said that he remained convinced that one day the Jewish people would come and save him. I believe that Mr. Sharansky wanted to transmit his enduring faith in the Jewish people to these children, who had been expelled from their homes by Israeli soldiers and felt betrayed by their own government. He had faith that he was part of a community of people who would not cease their efforts until he was released, a community of people he had never even met from places all around the globe, who cared enough to make sure he knew that he was never alone.

CREATING COMMUNITY

Rabbi Avraham Twersky warned my husband and me not to further isolate ourselves after our loss because we would lose the joy of connection to other people. He urged us to continue to go to weddings and celebrations, to continue to live.

Yet many people feel very alone when there is no community for them in hard times. Yvonne, a forty-six-year-old fashion designer, was married for sixteen years, and after her divorce nobody in the community invited her for the holidays, nor did they ask her to join them for Shabbat dinner. Nobody noticed that she felt abandoned, not just by her husband, but by the community as well.

Sometimes if there is a lack of community, you may be called upon to create one. And specifically because of what you have endured, you may be the person who can best be of service to others. Like Queen Esther in the Purim story, you are summoned to action. Queen Esther enjoyed private access to the king at the same time that his minister, Haman, was advising him to annihilate the Jewish people. It was she who had to persuade the king to rescind his orders. "Who knows if perhaps you were made queen for such a time as this," her Uncle Mordekhai reminds her.

By allying yourself with others in a community, you may find that your pain becomes a source of resilience for you and those around you. You have built compassion that allows you to be with others in their pain and loneliness – but, even more, to create a shared sense of hope.

QUESTIONS:
- What does the idea of community mean to you?
- Can you recognize a voice of inner kindness within you? What does that voice whisper to you?
- Describe a person or people who was/were kind to you. Who were they? How did they treat you? What did they say or do?
- Who have you been particularly kind to? How was that experience?
- What is a kindness you would like done for you? What is a kindness that you need?
- For what kindnesses can you thank your family?
- For what kindnesses can you thank God?
- What is your prayer for giving and receiving kindness?
- Is there anybody who has helped you by "deepening your pain"?
- Are you part of a community in your town or at work? Is there any community that you could join or create?

Chapter Three

Choice

"There is nothing so straight as a crooked ladder."
The Rabbi of Kotzk

The day that we found out that my son was murdered.... I don't like to think about that day. But I do know that in the afternoon I picked out the beret I would wear to the funeral. I'd been lying in bed crying, broken. I felt paralyzed, and that I wanted to die. I didn't know how we would live. I felt that the entire world had been destroyed, shattered. I thought that I would go out my door and the sky would be green, the grass blue, that the entire world would have rearranged itself.

For everyone else, it was the same world. Not for me. Not for my husband and kids. Yet, I remember choosing the color of the hat I would wear. I remember thinking to myself how disgusting I was to care, that I was so vain and ridiculous. Yet at the same time, I had an intuition that caring might save me. Choosing the color of a hat showed me that not all of my desire had been extinguished. Despite how shattered I felt, I was still alive.

In fact, even when it feels that you have no choice, there is still probably something that you can choose. You may choose to allow other people to help you. You may choose to look at others and yourself with a good eye, to appreciate what you have. Choosing will allow you to fare better in times of stress and trauma, when you feel that you have no control. But the more profound choice may be your ability to recognize God in your life – to believe that God is present in this pain. This enlargement, which may entail a revised understanding of the Divine, is a key component of resilience.

THE FREEDOM TO CHOOSE

One of the main tenets of Jewish theology is the notion of free choice. The first statement of God to man was a prohibition: You may not eat from the tree of good and evil. Yet Adam had the freedom to choose to disobey, to follow his own heart and the promptings of Eve. From the dawn of humanity, it has been our autonomy, our ability to choose, that defines us as free human beings.

God tells us, "I have placed before you life and death, blessing and curse, and you shall choose life" (Deut. 30:19). He urges us to choose what will be life-affirming, but the decision ultimately is in our own hands. Yet choice is complex and paradoxical because if God is omniscient, then He knows the chronology of our stories. Still, we have the freedom to choose our own plots, our own way of traveling through the stories of our lives. God does not need us to choose so that we determine the outcome of our stories. He wants us to choose so that we can refine our characters and personalities, so that we can become more like the Divine, more generous in spirit, able to create justice in the world, attentive to the needs of the weak and the needy.

Judaism continually stresses the primacy of choice. We even have the ability to choose and control our feelings. It takes work; it's not easy. We must prepare, but we can be responsible for our own emotions. For example, on Tisha B'Av we are enjoined to choose to feel sad, even if we fell in love the day before. On Purim, we are commanded to feel happy, even if we recently failed the bar exam. And on Shabbat, we are supposed to find peace, regardless of the emotional trials of the week that has just passed. One has to prepare oneself with study and actions to be able to transform one's feelings, so they correspond with the spiritual atmosphere of the day. Judaism is a religion that teaches us emotional maturity and control.

We often have help in achieving that maturity. For example, on the three major Jewish holidays, Sukkot, Passover, and Shavuot, we are supposed to feel happy. But how can a person be commanded to be happy? There is an answer: On these festivals, the Jewish people used to journey from their homes to gather at the Temple in Jerusalem. That meeting of people, that joining together, that feeling of community and caring generated happiness.

THE LIMITS OF CONTROL

Choice may provide a feeling of control, but sometimes the desire for control can undermine us. Too many choices can harm our decision-making. Professor Sheena Iyengar points out, for example, that in the supermarket, more than ten choices can paralyze a consumer's decision-making, and that an abundance of choices doesn't signify more freedom.

Furthermore, there are times we need to hesitate, to be less proactive, to step back and wait before choosing. In the *haftara* for Ḥanukka, God tells Zerubavel: "Not by physical might or power, but by My spirit, says the Lord of Hosts" (Zech. 4:6). In making choices, we need to differentiate between force and spirit (*koah* and *ruah*), and listen to our intuition so that we can sense the inner compass or spirit that is guiding us. Sometimes we need to persevere, to use the force of our will, in order to accomplish our goals. But sometimes all of that energy will be of little use. In that case, we are better off holding off, waiting for direction, surrendering to not knowing. Often, for example, when writing, I find that rather than forcing myself to keep working, it may be best for me to stop, go for a walk, or cook a meal, and suddenly an idea is called into my mind. Suddenly there is clarity.

Choice can protect us psychologically, especially in times of trauma – even when it cannot save us. During the Gaza War in the summer of 2014, we were told to plan how we would shield ourselves and our children in case of a missile attack: After hearing the warning siren, we should run into a shelter, or if we were driving, pull our cars over to the side of the road, and lie on the ground with our arms folded over our heads. After the tragic murder of twenty-seven children and staff at the Sandy Hook Elementary School in Newtown, Connecticut, one expert told parents to discuss with their own frightened kids steps they could take in the event of a shooting or other tragedy. For example, the children could hide under the desks or teacher's table if they were in danger. They could also try to call home. Knowing that they could choose a protective behavior (even one not guaranteed to rescue them from harm) gives children a resource for coping with the fear and horror of tragedy.

Psychologist Albert Bandura, a professor at Stanford University who studied self-efficacy, a perceived sense of control, confirms that "a large body of research has shown that perceptions of personal control are associated with a variety of positive outcomes, such as better physical and mental health, psychological well-being, and lower mortality."

According to Holocaust scholar Terrence Des Pres, female prisoners in Auschwitz who chose to care for their physical appearance as much as was possible in the concentration camps had higher survival rates than those women who had given up on self-care. Obviously women in concentration camps had very little control over their lives. Yet choosing simply to wash, an act of will and defiance, signaled a firm choice to maintain one's humanity and survive.

And then there are the times when no choice will protect us. When we lose a loved one, we know that we have no control and we are not in charge. But we may learn that in relinquishing control, we experience a different sense of choice. A story by the Maggid of Dubno (Rabbi Jacob Ben Zeev Kranz, born near Vilna in 1741) teaches us the secret of this process:

> Once there was a prince who wanted to become a master of archery. One day he happened to be passing through a village in the midst of an archery contest. He stopped to watch the marvelous skill of the contestants. One in particular had an uncanny knack for hitting the target. The prince asked for his secret. "Oh it's simple," the man answered. "First I shoot the arrow, and wherever it lands I paint the bull's eye around it."

I shoot the arrow, and wherever it lands I paint the bull's eye around it. We may feel that the arrow we sent into the world has missed the target that we were aiming at. But we have the power to move the target and paint the bull's eye around the mark our arrow has fallen on. We can extend our desire toward that for which we were not aiming. Then the events of our lives can be seen as a form of divine providence: Where we are is somehow where we need to be.

CHOOSING TO BELIEVE

Faith means that we include God in our story. Can we believe that God is leading us, even when it seems He is sending us incomprehensible troubles? Do we believe that God is guiding us even when the path is so dark it seems to be absolutely without illumination?

There are those who think that faith is not a choice, that some people magically feel God in their lives. But faith may be our most essential choice, one that has to be constantly renegotiated. As the Talmud says, "Everything is in the hands of God except for the fear of God" (Berakhot 33a).

Faith, *emuna* in Hebrew, is related to the word *imun*, training. One has to work at faith. It's not a gift that is granted but a muscle that needs to be constantly exercised and developed in an act of will.

Of course, it can be a challenge to believe in God. How can we believe in God's kindness when He has hurt us so? In fact, in his book *When Bad Things Happen to Good People*, Rabbi Harold Kushner argues that God absents Himself when something bad happens. For example, God had nothing to do with the Holocaust. It was caused by the will of evil people.

But I object to Kushner's argument. If God is not responsible, then God's power is limited, while according to traditional Jewish thought, God fills and activates the world. God is responsible even when a leaf trembles. God is the world but the world is not God. He is beyond our comprehension, the beginning and the middle and the end, the one who authors creation. His being transcends us at the same time that it fills us all.

If I find God in the midst of my sorrow, that helps me believe that God is present even in evil, and signals the possibility of a world that is greater than the one I can perceive. My suffering is not in vain. My child's death was not senseless. I don't understand it, but choosing to believe that it has significance means that God's world is more complex and vast and dimensional than my comprehension.

In order to recognize God in our suffering, we may choose to revise our understanding of God. According to Rabbi Joseph Dov Soloveitchik, an encounter with God is not only "great and blissful but also a shuddering and horror-filled experience."

When Moses went up to receive the Torah from God, "the appearance of the glory of the Lord was like a devouring flame" (Ex. 24:17). At Mount Sinai, when the Ten Commandments were given, the people saw the mountains shaking, on fire: "And the entire mountain shuddered exceedingly" (19:18). A midrash says that the souls of the people flew from them when God spoke. The experience of receiving the Torah was an experience of fire, a threat of annihilation in the face of the power of God. Rabbi Samson Raphael Hirsch says, "Godliness, taking up its home down here on earth, and wishing to be found down here, always announces itself as fire."

God isn't only present in tranquility. Unlike Greek philosophers such as Plato and Aristotle who perceived God in harmony and beauty, Judaism sees God as also present in chaos and catastrophe, when God communicates in what Rabbi Joseph Dov Soloveitchik calls the "covenantal" mode. Nature's cosmic mode follows an "unalterable order and sequence," a logic and beauty that are apparent, graspable, harmonious. The covenantal order, on the other hand, is an apocalyptic dialogue where God is present in the abyss, in the emptiness, in the *tohu* and *vohu*.

Four years ago, as a pastoral counselor, I worked with a woman at her baby's hospital bedside. She'd already lost a baby to a genetic disease, and her new baby was not given a good prognosis. She told me that she had always believed, always had faith. But after her baby died she realized that faith actually began when one's prayers hadn't been answered, when one's needs and longings had not been fulfilled, when one lost all feeling of control. Faith is achieved when one believes that God is compassionate and loving even when it seems the opposite – despite what our eyes witness in this world, that so often terrible things happen to innocent people who deserve better.

Judaism teaches us that God is an exacting, yet loving God. Many of the Hebrew texts and prayers stress God's love for us. "I have loved you, says God" (Mal. 1:2). The word love is mentioned twenty-three times in the book of Deuteronomy. "With a great love you have loved us, God," we say in the paragraphs preceding the morning *Shema*, the foundational Jewish prayer. In the *Shema* itself, we proclaim our obligation to love God: "And you shall love the Lord your God with all of your heart, with all of your soul, and with all of your might."

Yet we close our eyes in the beginning of the prayer. We distance ourselves from what we see only with our eyes – which may lead us astray. We remind ourselves that we should not evaluate God's love solely from the visual proof in this world, where moral justice is hard to apprehend.

APPRECIATION

The daily Jewish morning prayers remind us that we can choose to recognize the everyday blessings that surround us:

> Blessed are You God who gives sight to the blind.
> Blessed are You God who clothes the naked.

Blessed are You God who releases the bound.
Blessed are You God who straightens the bent.

It's not easy to choose to appreciate. The Torah itself can be read as a chronicle of complaints. After the Israelites, carrying the gold and silver bestowed on them by their Egyptian neighbors, witnessed the splitting of the sea as they left Egypt; after the signs and wonders of God's direct mercy and miracles in the wilderness; after being led by the pillar of cloud and the pillar of fire; the people complained of hunger in the desert: "If only we had died by the hand of God in the land of Egypt as we sat by the pot of meat, when we ate bread to satiety, for you have taken us out to this wilderness to kill this entire congregation by famine" (Ex. 16:3).

God fed them manna, a wafer-like substance bathed in honey that took on whatever taste the people wanted it to. And still, they could not stomach what they were given. Despite the wonders they had seen during the ten plagues, the Israelites were so embittered that Moses, their leader, was actually afraid that they would kill him in the desert.

The people were gifted with a direct experience of God's miracles and yet, as former slaves who had suffered deprivation and trauma, they could not endure the anxiety of the journey. They did not choose to appreciate their contact with the Divine.

But with support, we can choose to appreciate our lives. Paradoxically, loss can lead toward greater awareness of the everyday pleasures that surround us – the intricate design of a daffodil, the caress of hot water as we do the dinner dishes. Suffering can highlight the miracle in the mundane.

A GOOD EYE

In order to practice appreciation, we may choose to look with a good eye on our experience and separate the good from the bad.

This process is similar to the laws of the prohibition of *borer* or selection on Shabbat. On Shabbat, if we have a mixture of desirable and undesirable items, Jewish law teaches that we can separate the good from the bad. For example, if we have a bowl of popcorn that contains unpopped kernels we do not wish to eat, we separate the popped corn from them. This *halakha* is a sign that we can choose to focus on the good. It's not that the bad does not exist, rather we focus on the blessing that surrounds us.

This *halakha* can help us to re-envision our experience. For example, a few years ago, I was on line with my purchases in the *makolet*, the local grocery store, and a neighbor looked at me and said, "Whenever I feel bad about myself, I look at you. And then I don't feel so bad."

I was completely taken aback. I felt like she'd taken a pike and pierced me in the stomach. She was telling me that she comforted herself by knowing that she wasn't me, that her family hadn't undergone horror like mine. I returned home and told my children what had happened. My son who was eighteen at the time said to me, "She means that she respects everything you've done with Koby's murder, the foundation, the way you still smile and are happy. That it gives her hope."

When he told me that, I realized that I had a choice in how to interpret the hurtful comment. I could choose to look at it with a good eye, one that instead of condemning and judging, gives others and God the benefit of the doubt.

Mazal, a mother whose son Aharon suffered greatly and died at the age of twenty-four from leukemia, told me that after crying for more than a year, she had recently learned to bless God for the time that she had had with her son. I felt that her statement was a magnificent declaration. She was able to bless her time of mothering Aharon rather than only mourn what she had lost.

It sounds facile, but when we choose to turn a good eye, a loving eye, toward our lives and others, it means that we turn a loving eye toward ourselves. Our emotional life becomes less rigid and more expansive. We are less likely to be anxious, to blame, and to get hurt, more likely to appreciate other people, even if they make insensitive comments.

Moreover, in Jewish thought, the way we judge others influences the way that God judges us. The Baal Shem Tov explains that when it is written in Psalms that God is our shadow, it means that as we behave, so too He will behave toward us. If we judge ourselves and others with compassion, God will also be compassionate toward us. Yet even without ascribing compassion to God's intervention, it's apparent that when we choose to be kind, others are more apt to be kind to us.

For example, Dr. Joey Felder, a gastroenterologist at Mount Sinai Hospital in New York, says that choosing to be positive and hopeful can affect a person's health, although not always in terms of prognosis. "A good attitude won't help cure every disease. But, on the other hand, when a person chooses to be positive, the medical staff will pay more attention…because they will care more. They will want to be there more with the person," he explains.

It's like a law of physics. When we pay attention to the good in our lives, we call more good into our lives.

Appreciation is so important that the Talmud tells us that after the coming of the Messiah, the only sacrifice that will still be brought to the Temple will be the Thanksgiving offering.

SAYING AMEN AND AFFIRMING OUR EXPERIENCES

I once asked Butch Bradley, a comedian who performed in a Koby Mandell Foundation Comedy for Koby fundraiser, the secret of his brilliant improvisations. He told me, "It's the art of saying yes. I say yes to everything. It's like being a child. Oh, blue balloon, okay, I'll take that; Old City, yes, bus, yes, chair, yes, flag, yes."

When we say "amen" we are essentially saying "yes," affirming God's goodness. In Jewish practice, when you respond amen, you are supposed to say it as soon as possible after somebody else makes a blessing. Yet Jewish sources also mention an amen known as an "orphaned amen," recited long after the blessing is recited and therefore detached from the praise we are meant to be affirming. During the prayer services, such amens are to be avoided. In our lives though, when we are struggling with challenges, we may not be able to say amen to our experiences right away. But when we make the choice to interpret and explain those experiences in a positive way, we essentially say yes to our lives and give ourselves and others – our families and friends – the possibility of saying amen. We affirm that even in the midst of struggle and pain, God is present in our lives.

QUESTIONS:

- What is a choice that you made in the past that shaped your identity?
- What is a good choice that you made in your life? A bad choice?
- What choice would you change if you could?
- What did your parents teach you about making choices? If you have children, what do you tell them?
- What is a positive choice you can make today?
- What control do you have in your life today?
- What happens when you give up control?
- What is the difference for you between force and spirit in how you make decisions?
- How can you interpret your life in a more positive way?
- Was there a time that you had a clear sense of God's providence?
- What in your life do you say amen to? What do you wish that you could say amen to?
- Write a prayer for yourself where you choose to appreciate the beauty and kindness that surrounds you, to say amen.

Chapter Four

Creativity

"In every person there is something precious which
is in no one else. And so we should honor each for
what is hidden within him, for what only he has."
The Hasidic Masters

You have faced the chaos, entered your pain surrounded by a
community who has offered you kindness. You have chosen to
believe that the Divine is with you in this process of mourning,
yet you are still suffering. There is a crucial step that awaits you:
In order to mourn and be comforted, in order to transform your
pain, you need to engage your creative powers.

Creative activities, both playful and serious, can lead you
toward an enhanced sense of wholeness, health, and resilience.
It's telling that the root of the word creation (*bria*) in Hebrew
is also the root of the word for health (*briut*). By employing
the talents that are latent within us, our loss can paradoxically
compel us to realize our own vitality.

But be aware. There are different ways of creating from pain. When a precious vase shatters, there are those who throw out the pieces in despair. There are some who try to glue the fragments back together, even though they can never recreate the quality of the original vase. And then are those who create something new and unique from the shattered pieces. In fact, a Japanese ceramics technique, *kintsukuroi*, mends broken objects by filling the cracks with gold. And a broken vase, refashioned this way, looks, to many, even more aesthetically appealing. Artisans who practice this technique believe that objects which have been damaged have the potential for enhanced beauty.

We don't have to be ceramicists or dancers or writers or composers or playwrights or painters to create and renew ourselves. We may create a new family, have more children. We may remarry. And we can be artists of life: We may garden or cook or perfect lemon meringue pies or knit sweaters. A few weeks after Koby's murder, my kids and I spent a few evenings singing and drumming on overturned cooking pots. Our playful and original performances were a sign of the possibility of returning to emotional freedom.

RESHAPING THE SADNESS

Discovering and engaging with your own creativity is an urgent and essential task because it can protect not just you but your whole family and the generations to come. Dr. Ed Pakes, a psychiatrist from Toronto, says that 25 percent of psychiatric hospitalizations are due to unprocessed grief, pain that hasn't been expressed or dealt with in some way. And grief can be passed down through the generations. Author Scott Stossell, editor of *Atlantic* magazine, cites studies that demonstrate that anxiety is measurably higher in the children of second- and third-generation Holocaust survivors than in the general population.

In order to ensure mental health for you and your family, you may need not only to talk about your pain, to share it with others, but also to transform and process it into some new creation. In Hebrew the roots of the words for sadness (*etzev*) and design (*itzuv*) are the same. Sadness must be given shape.

When we feel that part of us is missing, that the world has lost its wholeness, that we suffer from a dissonance that cannot be reconciled, creating can help restore a sense of integrity. When we create, we enter our disturbance in order to search for meaning, harmony, and wholeness. We struggle to discern order hidden in our own personal chaos, the coherence that waits to be revealed in our suffering. Though we begin in pain, the creative process is one of intense life.

Suse Lowenstein's twenty-one-year-old son Alexander was killed on Pan Am flight 103 over Scotland in 1988. In the months following the bombing, Lowenstein worked on sculptures of Alexander to help return him to wholeness in her mind. Lowenstein also created a monumental sculpture in her backyard in Montauk, New York. *Dark Elegy* comprises seventy-five oversized stone figures of women frozen in the position of hearing the tragic news of their loved ones' deaths in the Lockerbie tragedy. You can see the pain and terror locked into the women's postures. Yet the women are arranged in a circular formation that transmits a sense of beauty and coherence in the midst of destruction.

Iris Yihichya's daughter, Yafit, a beautiful young woman who was then thirty-one and the mother of two small children, was murdered by a Palestinian terrorist on Moshav Mekhora in the Jordan Valley in August 2002.

Four months later, Iris attended a healing retreat run by the Koby Mandell Foundation. During the art therapy, she initially just sat. Then she began to work on a collage. She titled it *A Taste of the World to Come.*

When the art therapist asked to collect her work, Iris said no. Instead, she took the picture home and since then has been drawing, painting, and framing her work. By framing her art, she has been able to create symbolic borders around her suffering. Art is a means for her to express and contain and transform the longing and suffering that threaten to overwhelm and destroy her.

CREATING A NEW SELF

In the face of adversity, the recreation of self may be our most creative act.

Following a loss, we may discover a clarity, the ability to discern and separate, to distinguish between what and who is healthy and healing for us, those relationships and activities that will help nurture and build us and those that don't contribute to a life of greater meaning. In this process, we may discover a new being, a stronger sense of identity, new priorities. The ability to say "no." The ability to strive for loftier, more important goals. The ability to be truer to ourselves.

We may discover our most essential selves and in doing so, create a more profound relationship with the world. We may take risks that we would never have assumed in our past lives. Many of the mothers tell me: "I lost my child so what else is there to be afraid of?"

I personally dared to do things that I never would have considered before my son's murder. I, who was shy, began to speak out. Losing my son drove me to discover my voice. I spoke out at a Town Hall Meeting with Ted Koppel broadcast from Jerusalem. I confronted the Palestinian representatives on the panel, questioning why they taught hate in their schools and mosques and on their TV stations, and why they celebrated death. It's not that I had no fear. I did. But I was committed to my mission of honoring my son. I, who was afraid of audiences, began to speak around the world. I, who could hardly speak Hebrew before, spoke on Israeli television. I was compelled to tell my son's story. It was as if I became a different person, one who was more outspoken and courageous.

INSIGHT INTO A NEW SELF

Creativity allows us to discover the light hidden in our pain, the possibility of insight and revelation. God's first creation, when the world was still defined by its chaotic state, was light: "In the beginning of God's creating the heavens and the earth. And the earth was desolate and void, with darkness upon the surface of the deep – and a breath of God hovered over the surface of the waters. And God said let there be light" (Gen. 1:1–3).

As I wrote my book *The Blessing of a Broken Heart*, I began to understand that I had traversed the chaos and discovered a pattern hidden there. I began to write in chaos and despair and sadness three months after my son's murder, grappling with the shattering loss, the desolation and emptiness, as well as the traumatic cruelty of my son's murder. At first, my only goal was to remember my son. As I wrote, it was as if he were present. I could hear his voice whispering to me, deep inside me. I wanted to tell his story. I wanted to write my memories of him.

During that first year, as I wrote, I experienced several mysterious and powerful encounters: birds crashing dead at my feet when I walked in Jerusalem, hitting the windshield of my car, bouncing off of the headlights. I was confronted with a recurring enigma. What did birds have to do with my loss? As I researched and wrote, these encounters with birds and birds' nests gave me hints of transcendence, images of rising above the painful limits of this world. After a while, I realized that the book could be divided into two sections, the cave and the bird's nest.

The symbol of the bird's nest became for me the reverse image of the dark and isolated cave where my son was murdered. While the cave was impossible to exit, the bird's nest emerged as a place of birth and nurturing, a repository for light. That division provided a sense of order and harmony when the world seemed to me to be full of evil and chaos.

I still felt deep anguish but it was accompanied by hints of coherence. Later I learned that, according to the Kabbala, the Messiah waits in a bird's nest in the mystical Garden of Eden, poised to redeem the world. Furthermore, in that nest are images of the First and Second Temples as well as images of all of the children who have died sanctifying the name of God.

I was granted revelation when I decided to investigate the meaning of what I otherwise might have overlooked or disregarded. In my search for insight, I paved a path of healing, my own process of bibliotherapy. By tracing an arc of revelation in my book, I was able to compose a parallel narrative of coherence alongside the one of chaos, terror, and grief, the utter desolation and destruction. I understood that I could stay in the cave with the barbaric death of my son. Or I could choose to frequent the bird's nest, a place of healing, redemption and rebirth. I was no longer just a victim. I was a survivor, a spiritual detective, a person who was still capable of thriving.

DWELLING WITH GOD

The appearance of God at Mount Sinai was a traumatic experience for the People of Israel. They trembled in fear when they heard the thunder and lightning, and saw the mountain in smoke.

Even after hearing the word of God, the people apparently still did not have faith in His protection. Moses ascended to receive the rest of the Torah, but the people worried when his return was delayed, and they panicked. When Moses returned from his meeting with God, carrying the Tablets of the Law, he witnessed the people reveling in front of the Golden Calf, an idol of their own making. In his anger and disappointment, Moses smashed the tablets so they broke into pieces.

Moses later went back to God and returned with a new set of Tablets that he himself had carved. But what is most striking in the narrative is that both sets of Tablets, the pieces of the broken and the whole, were carried in the *Aron Kodesh*, the Holy Ark, and later found a home in the Temple. The broken tablets were not denied or discarded. Instead they were housed in the *Mishkan*, the Tabernacle, God's dwelling. God insists that our shattering be preserved.

All of us are composed of the broken and the whole. We need not avoid or overlook the shattered parts of our psyche. Instead, our intimate experience of the shattering may be the very force that compels us to rebuild. When we create from our pain, when we recreate ourselves out of both the whole and the broken pieces of our lives, perhaps we too can establish a sacred dwelling, a place of faith where the shattered can be given meaning, and where God is present in both our suffering and in our rebuilding.

ORIGINALITY

The word for light in Hebrew (*or*) is similar to the root of the word for waking. Rebbe Nachman of Breslov said that while many told stories to put people to sleep, he told stories to wake people up. This loss has awoken you toward a more inspired life.

In the morning *Modeh Ani* prayer, we thank God for renewing His creations daily, a sentiment echoed by the prophet Jeremiah, who proclaimed, with regard to God's continual acts of kindness to man, "They are new every morning, great is Your faithfulness" (Lam. 3:23). Every hour of the day offers us new experiences, a new vision, new creative opportunities through which to emulate the Creator as we redefine ourselves in our changed world. "The soul teaches constantly, but it never repeats," says R. Pinḥas, as quoted in Martin Buber's compilation, *Ten Rungs: Collected Hasidic Sayings*. Channeling our anxiety and pain into curiosity and play and creative work allows us to pay attention to moments of divine inspiration as we process and integrate our awareness and experience.

In the Koby Mandell Foundation mosaics class, our teacher Dana once told us that there are no mistakes in mosaics because everything can be woven into a design. By creating, you have found a way to weave this loss which feels so alien and foreign into a unique pattern that has its own surprising beauty. In seeking to express and comprehend and integrate what seems so mistaken, even random, you have discovered a unique personal vision that is a surprise, something you could not have planned or anticipated. This vision, which was hidden, can help guide you on your personal quest for resilience.

QUESTIONS:

- What did you like to do as a kid? What gave you pleasure?
- What does creativity mean to you?
- If you could do anything, what would it be?
- If you could create anything, what would it be?
- What have been the most creative moments of your life?
- What did your loved one like to create? Can you follow in his or her path?
- How do you give sadness shape?
- How have you been recreated as a result of sadness or struggle?
- What is your personal prayer for awakening your own sense of creativity?

Chapter Five

Commemoration

"Forgetfulness leads to exile, while remembrance is the secret of redemption."

The Baal Shem Tov

In 2012, the widows of the Israeli athletes who had been murdered in Munich in 1972 requested a moment of silence at the official opening of the summer London Olympics to commemorate the fortieth anniversary of the massacre.

The International Olympic Committee refused to allow the moment of silence, an official, shared commemoration, though they held an alternative ceremony off-site in London. Many people were angered at the Olympic Committee's response. The lesson of remembering the tragic consequences of hatred – the massacre of a group of eleven Jewish athletes by Palestinian terrorists – was not transmitted.

That omission was particularly painful because Judaism is a religion that insists on the primacy of remembrance. In his book *Zakhor: Jewish History and Jewish Memory*, Jewish historian Professor Yosef Yerushalmi teaches that the verb "to remember" is repeated 169 times in the Torah. In addition, the daily morning prayers conclude with six remembrances from the Jewish people's collective history. These verses describe events that are accompanied by a biblical injunction to remember, or not to forget, such as the Exodus from Egypt, the Giving of the Torah, and the sanctity of the Shabbat.

We're commanded to remember because it is so easy to forget. When things are good, we forget the challenges and heartache. In *Zakhor*, Yerushalmi says, "If the command to remember is absolute, there is, nonetheless, an almost desperate pathos about the biblical concern with memory, and a shrewd wisdom that knows how short and fickle human memory can be."

In this chapter, we will see that commemoration, a mindful act of remembering, is a means of creating a strong identity not only for a nation but also for families and individuals. The way we remember can obscure the past and paralyze us – or it can protect us and motivate us so that we become more caring, ethical people as a result of our history. By remembering, we transmit the past to our children, creating a continuity of longing and belonging. By passing on our stories of suffering and redemption, shame and praise, we continue to expound on and expand the Jewish story into a future time when others will tell the story for us. Recognizing that we are part of that story, which is larger than our individual lives, creates both personal and national resilience.

JUSTICE AND GRATITUDE

Commemoration, a dialogue with the past, has the power to help motivate us toward ethical behavior. In the postscript to *Zakhor*, Yosef Yerushalmi recounts a poll in the French newspaper *Le Monde*, in which readers were asked whether Nazi criminal Klaus Barbie should be indicted and put on trial. The question was phrased in this way: "Of the two following words, forgetting or justice, which is the one that best characterizes your attitude toward the events of the period of the war and occupation?"

As a result of the language of that poll, Yerushalmi realized that the antonym of forgetting may not be remembering but justice. In order to continually seek justice we have to actively remember.

The Bible abounds with verses commanding the Jewish people to remember that they were slaves in Egypt, and expecting them, as a result of that suffering, to be more compassionate, and to seek justice and equality. Rabbi Joseph Soloveitchik notes that ethics are not born in tranquility. Our pain – and others' – is what allows us to internalize ethical behavior, not just intellectually, but with our entire beings, to embody such behavior, and not just admire it.

Memory may also animate gratitude. It is Aaron, not Moses, who inflicts the first three of the Ten Plagues: blood, frogs, lice. A midrash tells us that Moses felt grateful to the river that had sheltered him when he was an infant, as well as to the sand that had covered the body of the Egyptian assailant whom he had killed. For that reason, he let Aaron initiate those plagues that involved water and the dust of the earth.

PROTECTIVE MEMORIES

Because memory can be unreliable, it is subject to more interpretation than most of us realize. Thus, it is quite easy to distort memory. Think of the Hebrew people in the desert complaining about the wonderful life they had had in Egypt: "If only we had died by the hand of God in the land of Egypt, as we sat by the pot of meat, when we ate bread to satiety" (Ex. 16:3). Though the Israelites were slaves who had never enjoyed such a feast they nevertheless romanticized the memories of the past because their journey through the desert was so fraught with peril and anxiety.

No memory is an exact replica of experience. Professor Antonio Damasia, a neurobiologist from the University of Southern California explains:

> There are no permanently held pictures of anything, no microfiches or microfilms, no hard copies.... When we recall a given object, or face, or scene, we do not get an exact reproduction but rather an interpretation, a newly reconstructed version of the original. As our age and experience change, versions of the same thing evolve. Memory is essentially reconstructive.

As a result, we have the opportunity to reconstruct our personal histories. I don't mean that we should distort or deny past memories. But we can highlight and create *preferred* memories, those that sustain and support us. We may choose not to be victimized by harmful experiences. We have the possibility of creating a cluster of "surround events," protective memories that motivate, mobilize, and liberate us.

I'm reminded of a contest at Camp Koby in which high school boys took turns tossing raw eggs from the second story of a building. First they wrapped the eggs in tape or towels to protect them. Similarly, we can find a way to enclose our memories with protective cushioning, thoughts that nourish rather than shatter us.

Gerda Weissmann Klein employed a protective memory to help her survive the Holocaust. As I mentioned, her parents and brother were killed during the war and she endured slave labor in a series of camps. When she met her husband, the United States soldier who liberated her, she weighed sixty-eight pounds and hadn't bathed in three years. In her memoir *All But My Life*, she describes how memory helped protect her in the camps:

> I was fortunate to have had a happy childhood, one that in all probability was not as perfect as I have chosen to remember. But its memory has helped me survive, and I have used it as a beacon to illuminate the darkness of the tragedy that followed.... The living room of my childhood. My father smoking his pipe and reading the evening paper, my mother working on her needlepoint, my brother and I doing our homework.... An evening at home. How many times I saw that picture...

Klein's ability to evoke the peaceful memories of her childhood helped her survive the cruelty of her experience in the camps. As she realizes, her home life may not have been as idyllic as she described, but the memory of the comfort and love she received from her family served as an antidote, a reverse image, of the nightmare she was living.

One of the powers of Camp Koby is the opportunity for children to form protective memories that nourish them. One summer day at Camp Koby, Shemaya, a seventeen-year-old counselor, told my husband and me about Tomer, a ten-year-old camper, who had become unusually agitated when a fellow camper was injured. Tomer's father had died of injuries from a car accident, and the sight of his friend lying on the field reminded him of the terrible days of his dad's coma. Shemaya continued to relate:

> I didn't know what to say, I felt so bad. But then I thought of something I'd learned in the counselor training. I said to him, "Can you tell me about your father? What did your father like to do?" He said, "Sailing. Playing sports, especially basketball." I asked him, "Do you want to go play basketball with me, right now?" We went to the basketball court and started to play. Tomer said, "My father said that you put your hands on the ball like this." After that we went to the basketball court every night together, with Tomer coaching me the way his father had taught him.

Shemaya not only gave Tomer a positive way of remembering his father – he also empowered Tomer to embody his father. Tomer was able to transmit his father's teachings, his voice. Tomer's memory of pain may well now be surrounded with loving memories, both of his father and of his counselor.

KEEPING THE MEMORY

Almost everybody who loses somebody is afraid that their loved one will be forgotten, erased from memory. I recently received an e-mail from a mother who is terrified that her thirty-two-year-old daughter who died of cancer will be forgotten.

One way of remembering is to create your own ritual of commemoration as a means of enabling and enacting memory. My husband learns a tractate of Talmud every year in honor of Koby. For the first five years after Koby's murder, we would go into Jerusalem on his birthday and give out money to beggars according to how old he would have been. For example, on his fifteenth birthday we gave money to fifteen beggars.

These acts of commemoration, beyond keeping our son's spirit alive for us, have enlarged our story. My friend Limor went to an orphanage and distributed fifteen toys for Koby's birthday. A woman who read my book decided to do the same on the anniversary of the death of a child she had been close to. A young girl I met, Hindy, distributed eighteen rolls in Machane Yehuda, the main outdoor market in Jerusalem, for her own birthday after reading my book.

The Danish writer Isak Dinesen said that there's no sorrow that can't be borne with a story. But I believe that it's not just telling the story that heals. It's also how others are changed by remembering the story, the actions that reverberate as a result of the story. The way we and others remember and commemorate can destroy or revitalize, constrict or expand us.

THE STORY OF THE FAMILY AND THE NATION

Within families, shared stories are important not only because they are interesting, but also because they convey memory. And the more we share our stories with our children and grand-children, the more they are aware of their family history, the more resilient they become.

Sara Duke, a psychologist who worked with children with learning challenges in the 1990s, noticed that the children who knew a lot about their families tended to fare better when faced with difficulty. Her husband, Professor Marshall Duke at Emory University, decided to test this hypothesis. He and his colleague Robyn Fivush developed a measure called the *Do You Know* scale, twenty questions which they used to survey children. Questions included ones like: "Do you know where your grandparents grew up? Do you know where your parents met? Do you know where your parents went to high school? Do you know of an illness or something terrible that happened in your family?"

In his study, he found that "the more children knew about their family's history, the stronger their sense of control over their lives, the higher their self-esteem, and the more successfully they believed their families functioned." He concluded that "the *Do You Know* scale turned out to the best single predictor of children's emotional health and happiness."

After 9/11, the researchers assessed a set of children who, while not directly affected, had experienced the same national trauma. They again found that "the ones who knew more about their families proved to be more resilient, meaning they could moderate the effects of stress." In addition, those who were told stories of both victories and defeat, an oscillating narrative, proved to have the greatest measure of resilience. These children know that challenges, losses, and failures are part of life, as is success, victory, and happiness.

The power of the narrative of the family of Jewish people – a bridge across generations – may be a key factor in our startling national resilience. We tell and retell our collective story, forging our national identity. Jewish life is a continual transmission of our history, an ongoing conversation. We build sukkot during the fall in order to commemorate our ancestors' pilgrimage in the desert; we feast on Purim in order to remember Queen Esther's victory over the Persians. We read from the Torah portion of the week to animate history and memory; each Shabbat, indeed each day, we remember our exodus from Egypt. We remember so that we are changed, affected, moved, motivated, mobilized, united. Ritual, prayer, and holiday celebrations span time as both retrospective and anticipatory performances.

And we tell a story that describes both the weaknesses and the strengths in our national history, a fluctuating narrative of both victory and defeat. For example, the narrative arc of the Passover Haggada is a movement from ignominy to praise – from being slaves who served Pharaoh to becoming free people who can worship and praise God.

We tell our national story so that we can transmit the wisdom of our history. We are part of a larger story that started before us and will continue after us, and the more that we know and identify with that story, the stronger our connection to our heritage, the more resilient we are as a nation. During Operation Protective Edge in Gaza in the summer of 2014, a Hamas member who was interviewed in Gaza said that the Jewish people would not have the will to be able to survive a protracted battle. How little he knew about the strength and continuity of our national resolve, forged by the collective narrative of the Torah, fortified by ritual and holidays and by our continual remembrance.

ETERNITY

In Hebrew the word for commemorate contains the word for eternity (*netzah*). When we commemorate, when we remember, we are able not only to transfer knowledge, embody a loved one, inspire ethical behavior, or forge national identity, but even to transcend the bounds of time. The concept of eternity contributes to a deeper understanding: Death does not necessarily sever all of our connections with our loved ones.

Freud believed that mourning was successful when all ties with the person who had died were cut off. He called this process decathexis, the release of the emotional energy we had invested in the person, the disconnection from the loved one. In other words, our relationship with the loved one ends when he dies.

But we see in our own work at the Koby Mandell Foundation, and many psychologists confirm, that there is still a chance for a connection, even with somebody who is physically gone.

Nancy Vilaboy, a pastoral counselor at a large senior residence in Cincinnati, experienced that connection in a powerful way last Mother's Day. Her only son, a young man in his twenties, had died of cancer a year earlier. While she was at work, a volunteer said, "Happy Mother's Day" and then put her arm on Nancy's hand and said, "Oh that's right, you're not a mom anymore." Nancy says that she had to draw deeply on God's grace to walk away from that remark. But the same day she received a sign of connection from her son:

> Mother's Day was a day that I really struggled with this year and as I was talking to my son, I said, "Chris, I know you send me signs all the time…but this year, I need you to let me know you hear my voice and that you are still close to me." I decided to sort through some old books to donate. As I opened one of those books, I saw something pink sticking out of it, and as I pulled it out, I realized it was a heart folded in two and, scrawled with my son's first-grade handwriting, were the words, "I LOVE YOU."

Of course we don't have the person back, the physical presence that we crave, and we can't rely only on signs. But if a bereaved family creates an ongoing intimacy with the person who died, it's often a sign of health, of resilience.

Professor David Pelcovitz of Yeshiva University cites a study of Israeli families who lost their husbands and fathers in the Yom Kippur War. In addition to the presence of photographs of the deceased, what distinguished the resilient families was the way that the mother was able to express her feelings, and cry in front of her children, incorporating the memory of the lost father into the mythic consciousness of the family, even if she had remarried. When she talked about the father, and told stories about him, it was as if he continued to be part of the family.

At Koby's *yahrtzeit* (memorial anniversary) last year, his friend, Shlomo, who was then twenty-six, shared a story about Koby's remarkable insight and sensitivity. Shlomo's father, Tuvia, who had been disabled or sick for much of Shlomo's life, died shortly before Koby's murder. At the *shiva*, Shlomo told Koby that he had hardly known his father. What Koby told him then was astounding: "You know what? You can still get to know him now. Ask your mother about him, ask others about him. Find out what their memories are. Take what's good about him and let those qualities live on in you." Koby was thirteen at the time.

I felt like this story was also a message for our family from Koby. A person can live on when we choose to embody them in their loving ways. We are not bound by the constraints of time. When we leap over the limits of time and create a living memorial, we touch eternity. Moreover, we continue a relationship with the person's soul, which is pure and enduring.

Rabbi Adin Steinsaltz once told me: "When people lose somebody, most make a memorial that is dead. But a memorial has to be living. When a tree dies, if you can't make that tree grow, you need to plant another tree."

Our choice to integrate our loved one's kindness and good qualities into our lives allows us to become living memorials. In one of the Koby Mandell Foundation's women's support groups we talked about the mothers' fear of forgetting their children. But one mother said that as a result of her son's death, she had internalized his positive qualities and become more truthful, more compassionate, and more powerful. As a result, she felt a vital ongoing connection to him: her whole self had been enlarged. That sense of expansion is a powerful sign of resilience.

QUESTIONS:

- What do you commemorate?
- What rituals have you built into your life?
- Which Jewish rituals are most meaningful to you?
- What is the meaning of commemoration for you?
- Can you identify positive memories that surround the painful ones of suffering?
- What family stories were passed on to you? What are the family stories that you tell to your own family?
- Do you feel a connection with the soul of the person who died?
- How can you create a living memorial?
- What is your personal prayer for remembering your loved one?

Chapter Six

Consecration

"For this is God, our God forever and ever. He will
guide us eternally."

Psalms 48:15

In the Torah, Joseph's brothers throw him into a pit and then
turn away and eat a meal while they abandon their brother for
dead. Twenty-two years later, the brothers journey down to
Egypt as the result of a famine. They don't recognize Joseph,
who is now the vice-regent of Egypt, the leader who will provide for them. When Joseph can no longer contain himself, he
tells them that he is their brother. Later in the story, after their
father, Jacob, dies, the brothers are afraid that Joseph will turn
on them for their cruelty to him. But he tells them not to worry
or be disturbed, because it was not the brothers who sent him
forth, but rather God. Joseph understands that he is part of a
mission, greater than either himself or his brothers.

When we see God's hand in our lives, we participate in an act of consecration: recognizing the sacred. In Hebrew the word holy contains the idea of separation, to be set apart for a special purpose. We who suffer sometimes feel that we are sundered from our loved one, set aside, alienated from others and our past. Yet as Rabbi Joseph Soloveitchik writes, all suffering is a summons. If in our suffering we discover a sense of mission, a special sense of enlarged purpose, we participate in repairing and redeeming the world, creating a lifeline of resilience.

BURNING WITHOUT BEING CONSUMED

God speaks to Moses from the midst of the burning bush, and the bush burns but is not consumed.

A midrash states that, along with Moses, there were many shepherds in the area, but not one stopped to view the burning bush. None had the curiosity or courage. Perhaps they were afraid, or distracted, or simply too involved with ordinary life. Moses turned to see, to look, to behold. And once he witnessed the burning bush, God spoke to him and told him that he was the one who would lead the Jews out of Egypt, from their slavery. Moses was told to take off his shoes, as the priests do when they serve in the Temple, as mourners do during a *shiva*. He had been called into divine service, received his sacred mission.

We ourselves have become burning bushes, suffused with loss. There are losses in our life that burn forever, yet we can burn without being destroyed. Most people are oblivious to this world of burning. So many bereaved people tell me that others ask them, "You're over it, right? I mean it's been a few years now."

But the burning bush is a symbol of hope for Moses and for the Jewish people throughout the ages, a message of resilience. Even when we fear that our personal loss may destroy us, the burning bush tells us that we will not only endure but will discover an impassioned and urgent mission, a sense of destiny.

THE PROCESS OF BECOMING

At the burning bush, when Moses asks what name he should use to refer to God when he returns to the Hebrew people, God says, "I will be what I will be." This name shows that God Himself is not fixed or static but is in a process of becoming.

We too are in a passage of becoming. Abraham Joshua Heschel says, "Creation, we are taught, is not an act that happened once upon a time, once and for ever. The act of bringing the world into existence is a continuous process. God called the world into being. That call goes on."

We have been called on to participate in the process of redeeming the world. It's not that we are special. Rather, we have become special. The bush that is on fire is seemingly an ordinary thorn bush, not a monumental sycamore or a verdant apple tree, but a plain bush covered in thorns. We too are ordinary people, ill-equipped for the fire of our pain, disbelieving that we can take this pain and convert it into a calling.

Even Moses has a hard time accepting the mission that God has demanded of him and questions his own ability to lead. He asks God: "Who am I that I should go to Pharaoh and that I should take the Children of Israel out of Egypt?" God answers him, "For I shall be with you" (Ex. 3:11–12).

God has granted us a mission of saving or repairing some part of the world. In this way, even though we may be fearful, we become fuller participants in God's unfolding story of redemption as we are drawn to mend the world, one stitch at a time.

POST-TRAUMATIC GROWTH

It's not just that we survive, we learn to thrive. Like the magnificent gigantic balboa tree that grows at the edge of the desert on Kibbutz Ein Gedi near the Dead Sea, we may absorb unique nutrients from an environment that others perceive as devoid of sustenance. One must have patience, but all of us are capable of becoming greater and flourishing, as we achieve a greater sense of purpose in the world.

As Rabbi Joseph Soloveitchik says with regard to suffering, "Man passes over the boundary of selfhood and becomes greater than he really was destined to be in the cosmic scheme of things." In *Letters to a Young Poet*, Rainer Maria Rilke tells Herr Kappus, his correspondent, "Do you remember how this life has longed ever since childhood for the great? I see how it is now longing to leave the great for greater. Therefore it does not cease to be difficult, but it will not cease, either, to grow."

It's clear that even if tragedy initially weakens us, it can motivate post-traumatic growth. According to an article in the *New York Times Magazine* about a 1980 study conducted on aviators captured during the Vietnam War, 61 percent felt they had benefited psychologically from their experience of captivity:

> Many said that they had stronger religious convictions and enjoyed life more. They said they appreciate others more. Those treated most harshly by their captors reported the most positive change. Perhaps it was no more than the desire to give meaning to a horrible time in their lives, but a follow-up study conducted twenty-five years later found that the soldiers remained convinced that the captivity had changed them for the better.

In the Torah, when King Balak asks Balaam, the non-Israelite prophet, to curse the Jews, he tries to do so three times, but each time the curse turns into a blessing. The Jewish people are the exemplars of post-traumatic growth. What could have destroyed us, as a curse, has become instead the source of blessing and enlargement. As Nietzsche said in his well-known maxim: "That which does not destroy me, makes me stronger."

DESTINY

In *Pirkei Avot, Ethics of the Fathers*, we learn: "Who is the wise man? He who learns from everybody" (4:1). Even this loss, this trauma, this unwanted visitor in your life, even this has become a teacher, inspiring you to take action.

You are no longer the victim of impartial circumstances, fickle and unpredictable, accidental. The fate that you unwittingly have fallen into has now been integrated and assimilated so that your experience is woven into a sense of destiny.

Rabbi Soloveitchik speaks about the difference between fate and destiny: "Man's task in the world, according to Judaism, is to transform fate into destiny; a passive existence into an active existence, an existence of compulsion, perplexity and muteness into an existence replete with a powerful will, with resourcefulness, daring and imagination."

Tikkun olam, repairing the world, comes from a place of deep pain and struggle. We no longer stand mute in the face of chaos. We seek the repair, shift, or disclosure that is only possible because of what we have undergone. It's as if you have been granted a personal prophecy that serves to rally and mobilize you.

But that sense of mission, that personal prophecy, can also inspire and motivate others. Therefore, it is imperative that we share our stories. On Israel Memorial Day one year, my husband spoke in Toronto at a Jewish Community Center, and his story affected a group of boys in a stunning and powerful way.

This is the story that Seth shared:

> A few days after Koby's funeral, boys from his eighth-grade class came to visit us during the *shiva*. There was one boy, very shy, short, pale. A bigger boy, at least a head taller, pushed him forward. "He has something he wants to tell you," he said gruffly.
>
> The boy shuffled forward and began to speak almost in a whisper. "I'm not very good in sports," he said. "And Koby was very good. He was one of the best in the class. At the end of gym class last week we were supposed to divide into volleyball teams. Koby was one of the captains, he had first choice. I was always the last person to be chosen. And Koby chose me."

Seth continued:

> Koby loved to win. He was the most competitive person I know. But Koby picked the boy that nobody else wanted on their team.
>
> When we first moved to Israel, Koby didn't have any friends. He couldn't speak Hebrew. He was an outsider, a nerd, even though he had been very popular in his class in Silver Spring. So he could understand his classmate's humiliation. He was able to see what was really important.

Then Seth added: "Sometime in the next twenty-four hours you are going to have a chance to do the right thing, and when you do, think of Koby and the kindness he did. And make the right choice."

At the end of his lecture, a high school boy approached Seth. "I'm Michael," he said. "I didn't come to hear your speech. I came to play basketball. But I stuck my head in and I heard what you said about Koby and the volleyball story. I'm like Koby, one of the best players in the class. And I really liked your story about Koby. I decided that next time I'm captain, I'm going to change who I pick."

Seth got on the plane, came home from Toronto. He never expected to hear from Michael, but a few days later he got an e-mail from him:

> Rabbi Mandell, I am not sure if you remember me, but I'm the high school boy who came up to talk to you after your speech. The very next day in gym class, I was the captain. I picked the worst boy in the class for my basketball team. His face lit up. Then when I saw how happy he was, I picked the next worst player. Again he smiled like crazy. So I picked the next worst athlete in the class. I had a team of the very worst players. We played a round robin tournament that day. And I don't know how we did it. I really don't. But we won the basketball tournament – every game. I wish you could have seen the smiles on the boys' faces. They could have lit up the world. They were thrilled. I've never been so happy.

I imagine that in shaping his team the way he did, Michael helped mend a small piece of the world: those boys' fragile sense of self-worth. He also may have revised his own view of competition. Those boys shared a beautiful victory because my husband shared our story.

My husband and I created the Koby Mandell Foundation in 2001 because we understood from our own children that kids needed their own space and time to share their pain and joy. After Koby's death, our children suffered because there was nowhere for them to turn. They didn't want to bother us because they could see that we were broken. They didn't want to cry to us. Also, children's grief is different from that of adults. Children can cry and then play right afterwards. If the children don't cry, often the parents or remaining parent assumes that they are okay. But children often suffer as the silent victims of bereavement. No camp for bereaved children existed so we built Camp Koby and in the last fourteen years have helped thousands of children. One boy who came to Camp Koby told me, "I thought I was the only one." We are able to relieve the children's isolation and allow them to express their hidden suffering – as well as their joy.

Once you have been inspired to take on a serious project, you are more likely to be infused with an ongoing sense of mission. You understand that you don't have to stand by, but can instead confront injustice. In the summer of 2013, the week before a group of prisoners was to be exchanged in a "good will gesture" intended to bring the Palestinians to the negotiating table, I was so angry at the prospect of more terrorist murderers being released that I became an activist and organized a protest all by myself. I'd never done such a thing before and I did it overnight, putting together a group on Facebook. Almost fifty people gathered in front of the Prime Minister's office to voice their disapproval of the government's policy.

Four months later, with a few other mothers who participate in Koby Mandell Foundation programs, I founded a political group, Forever Mothers, against the exchange of Palestinian murderers. In 2003, twenty-five-year-old Shira Avraham, another founding mother, witnessed her seven-month-old baby Shaked, then her only child, and her twenty-seven-year-old neighbor,

Eyal Yeberbaum, murdered in front of her eyes, when a terrorist, armed with a rifle, broke into her home on the evening of Rosh HaShana. Later, Shira and her husband learned that this terrorist had been released two months earlier in a prisoner exchange.

I organized a visit to the Knesset where twenty bereaved mothers and fathers spoke to Knesset members and the press. Our group organized a prayer service at Rachel's Tomb. A month later, I met with MK Tzipi Livni to protest the release of prisoners. I, who was embarrassed to speak Hebrew in ulpan, became an activist for a cause I believed was crucial.

Almost everybody whom our group spoke to about our mission told us that it was not going to work, that the Israeli policy of releasing prisoners would not change. But we said that we had to bring our voices to the conversation, regardless of the outcome. We insisted on speaking out. And in fact, the prisoner exchange was nullified.

There are so many people who go on to heal the world as a result of the deaths of loved ones. After the death of their daughter Marnie, a twenty-eight-year-old doctor who died of brain cancer, Jerry and Lainie Rose established the Dr. Marnie Rose Foundation in order to research pediatric brain cancer and support brain cancer patients and their families. As a result of research that their foundation funds, they have already seen progress in the survival rate of brain cancer patients.

THE STONE THE BUILDERS REJECTED

Sometimes that which hurt us can even become the instrument of our healing. In the book of Genesis, after the snake enticed Eve to eat from the Tree of Knowledge of Good and Evil, she and Adam were punished and expelled from the garden. They were then told to sew themselves clothes from the fig tree (and not, in fact, the apple tree as is commonly believed), the Tree of

Knowledge. That which had been an element in their downfall was now the agent of their protection.

In *Parashat Ḥukkat*, a similar process occurs: God sends fiery serpents to attack the Israelites in the desert because of their endless complaints, this time about the manna. But after the people repent and Moses prays, God tells Moses to craft a brass serpent. When the people look up at the brass snake, they are healed.

A few years ago, while I was on a vacation in Rhodes with my eighteen-year-old daughter and my friend Shira and her daughter, I had a comparable experience: something which had hurt me became an instrument of healing.

Before we left for Greece, I had read on the Internet that we wouldn't enjoy the hotel beach which was full of sharp rocks. But on our first morning there, Shira and I went for a walk on the beach and decided to lie on the hot rocks. Shira is a massage therapist, and she decided to try working with the hot rocks, to see if she could use them in her work. I lay on a lounge chair and agreed to let her experiment on me. Her hot rock massage felt extraordinary.

The fact that I could enjoy a hot rock massage was a surprise. My son was beaten to death with rocks; rocks are not on the top of my list of favorite things.

I was also surprised that I could enjoy a vacation. For years after Koby was killed, empty time filled me with trepidation because traumatic, ugly, violent thoughts of Koby's murder entered my mind. I couldn't feel a sense of peace or ease. But there I was on the hot rocks, and I felt relaxed and peaceful.

A few weeks after our trip, I told the story of the hot rocks to a group of high school girls at Camp Koby. I told them how I learned from this experience that you can take something hard and find a way to transform it into something good. That doesn't mean it doesn't hurt. In Judaism we are taught that everything God does is for the good, but when tragedy strikes, it is almost impossible to see that good. We feel only the pain.

The girls looked at me and one, whose brother had been murdered in a bus bombing, said, "You know there is also sometimes light in the rocks. You can rub two sticks together to make fire. But flint, a kind of rock, also has a spark."

In Psalms we read: "The stone the builders rejected has become the cornerstone" (Ps. 118:22). Sometimes what is most feared, most difficult, can be the place from where we build and repair. Everything has a spark of God in it says the Kabbala. And our job in the world is to gather those sparks, even from the hardest places, and enlighten the world with them. When we are moved to discover the holiness hidden in the darkness of our pain, we experience the power and brilliance of resilience.

QUESTIONS:
- What does holiness mean to you?
- Can you see God even in the midst of your pain?
- Has your mission in life changed? Have you found a sacred calling? A purpose?
- In what ways have you become greater as a result of your loss?
- What is your personal prayer for mending your portion of the world?

Epilogue

Celebration

"People imagine a place of godliness as a place for seriousness, a solemn place, a place that fills you with trepidation. The fact is, where there is God, there is joy."

The Lubavitcher Rebbe

At the close of a radio interview a few months ago, the host asked me, "I understand that after a loss, you have to find a new sense of normal. Is that true?" I thought about it and then answered her, "No, I don't think so. Normal isn't enough. One has to find a new extraordinary."

Resilience isn't bouncing back to a new normal. It's a heightened feeling of life, a sense of greater engagement and enlargement, an awareness and realization of the extraordinary.

"*Batzaar hirḥavta li* – In my distress you have relieved me," says King David (Ps. 4:2). But the word for relieved also conveys the meaning of broadening, extending. The Psalmist's words can be taken to mean: "In my narrow places, you have enlarged me. I have taken in this suffering and expanded with it."

We who have suffered and grown and flourished may experience a surprising sense of joy. If you were to visit Camp Koby, you would see that when bereaved children are happy, their joy is even greater than that of other children. One of our counselors described Camp Koby, perhaps surprisingly, as the happiest place she has ever been, a Garden of Eden on this earth.

In transcending our pain, in converting it into a mission, a destiny, we have experienced a tremendous breakthrough. We do not deny our sadness; it will always be present. Yet our sense of joy expands. We know that when we attend weddings and bar mitzvas we will cry, but we will laugh too. And our laughter will be a larger, truer laughter. For when one has tasted great sadness, the repertoire of one's emotions may expand. In that expansion, there is celebration and joy.

FEELING THE PRESENCE OF GOD

At Mount Sinai, the people received the Torah according to each one's ability to bear the voice of God. When the Torah was given, all the people "saw" the voices: "The entire people saw the voices and the flames, the voice of the shofar and the smoking mountain" (Ex. 20:14). Not the voice but the voices. The Midrash explains this:

> R. Tanḥuma said: "How did the voice come forth for Israel? According to the strength of each individual Israelite, according to what he could hear.... So it says: "The voice of God is in strength." According to the strength of each individual.... Said R. Yossi bar Ḥanina: "If this surprises you, learn from the manna which fell for the

Israelites in the wilderness; its taste was adapted so that each individual should be able to bear it…if this was so with the manna, how much more so with the voice of God, that it should not cause injury." (*Pesikta DeRav Kahana* 12:25)

The people heard God's voice according to what they were capable of absorbing. We who have suffered may experience an enlarged capability to see and hear and recognize God in both our suffering as well as in the ordinary blessings of our days. The biblical Jacob realizes that "God was in this place, and I did not know it" (Gen. 28:16) only after he flees his brother Esau who has threatened to kill him. Stopping on his journey, he dreams of a ladder stretching to heaven on which angels of God are ascending and descending. God reveals himself, saying: "Behold, I am with you" (Gen. 28:15).

Abraham Joshua Heschel says, "Every moment is [God's] subtle arrival and man's task is to be present." Chaos, *tohu* in Aramaic, means "Why?" With the plunge into the great mystery of mortality and meaning and darkness, you have been emboldened to profoundly question, to change, to grow larger, to express what was there waiting but concealed.

You have experienced an expanded sense of God's presence, in sadness and in happiness. For you are aware that the *tohu*, the chaos and despair and confusion that you have endured, is not only desolation and nothingness. It is not the absence of God but rather God's presence, a vast expanse where you were pushed and prodded and propelled to develop your hidden capacities and create and build, to discover your destiny, to forge identity, and repair the world.

In that germination and development, in that flowering, there is joy.

HUMANITY, VULNERABILITY, AND JOY

We experience joy not only in our expansions but in realizing the true nature of existence. One of the happiest holidays in Judaism, Sukkot, is a time of joy where we also recognize our own vulnerability. During that week, we build temporary huts as the Jewish people did when they were traveling in the desert in biblical times. This holiday period is referred to as "the Time of our Happiness."

We eat and sleep in huts built with three walls, whose roofs must be open to the stars, permeable. Sukkot teaches that our dwelling on this earth is temporary and insecure. When we live outside, we leave not only our comforts but our feelings of permanence. We can't lock our sukka, and we are vulnerable to the sun, the rain, winds, animals.

But there is great joy in being in a sukka. We are out of our routine, out of our homes, exposed. In the Zohar, the sukka is referred to as the "shadow of faith" (Zohar 103a). Those of us who have dwelled in loss know that we are vulnerable, but we are also privileged to comprehend our true human condition, our humility and impermanence. Sukkot teaches us that this world is like a sukka, the World to Come the world of eternity.

THE SONG OF JOY

I look at the line from Psalms, expressed in the plural, "They who sow in tears will reap in song" (Ps. 126:5). And I finally understand: You can't do this alone. You are not meant to be alone. We are here to support and help and teach and heal each other, and God is with us. Our pain is part of being human – every one of us has to lose those we love. But the pain is also part of God's wish for us to become greater, His yearning for humanity to act with loving-kindness and justice.

When we join together in our task of repairing this world, when we have the faith and the courage to continue sowing together even in the midst of pain, we are promised that we will be blessed with great joy that will find expression in shared joyous song. The wordless cry of pain we began with will be transformed into prayer and then, praise and song.

Rabbi Abraham Isaac Kook, the first chief rabbi of Israel, writes:

> There is one who sings the song of his soul. And there is one who sings the song of his people. Then there is one whose soul expands until it extends beyond the border of Israel, singing the song of all humanity...there is one who expands even further until he is united with all of existence, with all creatures, with all worlds, with the universe, a song that encompasses all.

You are no longer imprisoned in your suffering, in the small place of ego, a narrow mind, a limited consciousness. You have expanded your view to identify with all of God's creatures and become greater. You do not deny suffering, but help to alleviate it; you do not ignore another person's pain, but offer compassion. You help others discover their divine missions, their share in healing the world. You know that you are part of an ongoing divine chorus in which each person helps the others lift their voices so that all can harmonize in one great melody. Then each person's song sounds richest, purest, most true and most vital.

The letters of the Hebrew word for Israel can be rearranged to form the words, God's song. From the midst of your pain you have discovered the spiritual art of resilience. Your life is now a song to God.

QUESTIONS:

- What joy did you feel in your family of origin?
- How did your family celebrate when you were a child? How do you celebrate now?
- What do you celebrate in life now?
- What celebration would you like to create in your life?
- How have you experienced a sense of enlargement?
- What sense of breakthrough have you experienced?
- How can you call more joy into your life?
- How have you converted your sadness into song?
- What is your personal prayer for joy?

Bibliography

Appelfeld, Aharon. *The Story of a Life*. Translated by Aloma Halter. New York: Schocken Press, 2009.

Buber, Martin. *Ten Rungs: Collected Hasidic Sayings*. New York: Schocken Press, 1947.

Des Pres, Terrence. *The Survivor: An Anatomy of Life in the Death Camps*. New York: Oxford University Press, 1976.

Diehl, Manfred, and Elizabeth L. Hay. "Risk and Resilience Factors in Coping with Daily Stress in Adulthood: The Role of Age, Self-Concept Incoherence, and Personal Control." *Developmental Psychology*. September 2010: 46.

Dobbs, David. "A New Focus on the Post in Post-Traumatic Stress." The *New York Times*, December 25, 2013.

Dykstra, Robert. *Images of Pastoral Care: Classic Readings*. St. Louis: Chalice Press, 2005.

Feiler, Bruce. "The Stories that Bind Us Help Children Face Challenges." The *New York Times*, March 17, 2013.

Fromm, Erich. *The Art of Loving*. Bantam: New York, 1963.

Heschel, Abraham J. *Between Man and God: An Interpretation of Judaism*. New York: Simon & Schuster, 1959.

Hollander Goldfein, Bea, Jennifer Goldenberg, and Nancy Isserman. *Transcending Trauma: Survival, Resilience, and Clinical Implications*. New York: Routledge, 2011.

Hyde, Lewis. *The Gift*. New York: Vintage Books, 2007.

Klein, Gerda Weissmann. *All But My Life*. New York: Hill and Wang, 1957.

Kook, Rabbi Abraham Isaac. *Lights of Return*. Translated by Dr. Alter B.Z. Metzger. New York: Yeshiva University Press, 1978.

Kramer, Chaim. *Crossing the Narrow Bridge: A Practical Guide to Rebbe Nachman's Teachings*. Jerusalem: Breslov Research Institute, 1989.

Levinas, Emmanuel. *Nine Talmudic Readings*. Bloomington: Indiana University Press, 1990.

Pressburger, Chava, ed. *The Diary of Petr Ginz 1941–1942*. New York: Grove Press, 2004.

Rilke, Rainer Maria. *Letters to a Young Poet*. New York: Dover, 2002.

Sacks, Rabbi Jonathan. *To Heal A Fractured World: The Ethics of Responsibility*. New York: Schocken, 2005.

Sacks, Oliver. *An Anthropologist on Mars*. New York: Vintage, 1995.

Seligman, Martin. *Flourish: A Visionary New Understanding of Happiness and Well-being*. New York: The Free Press, 2012.

Soloveitchik, Rabbi Joseph Dov. *Out of the Whirlwind: Essays on Mourning, Suffering and the Human Condition*. New Jersey: Ktav, 2003.

Stern, Esther. *Just One Word*. Jerusalem: Feldheim, 2005.

Stossell, Scott. *My Age of Anxiety: Fear, Hope, Dread, and the Search for Peace of Mind*. New York: Knopf, 2014.

Yerushalmi, Yosef. *Zakhor: Jewish History and Jewish Memory*. New York: Schocken, 1989.

Zornberg, Avivah Gottlieb. *The Beginning of Desire: Reflections on Genesis*. New York: Doubleday, 1996.

—. *The Murmuring Deep: Reflections on the Biblical Unconscious*. New York: Schocken, 2009.

The fonts used in this book are from the Garamond family

Other works by Sherri Mandell

The Blessing of a Broken Heart

The Toby Press publishes fine writing
on subjects of Israel and Jewish interest.
For more information, visit www.tobypress.com.